M000234358

# WORD
# SAVVY
*Handbook*

## Use the Right Word

NANCY RAGNO

ISBN: 9781733928700

Library of Congress Control Number: 2019911310

BISAC: Language Arts & Disciplines
        LAN000000; LAN22000; LAN006000

Dewey Decimal Classification: 425

CONTACT INFORMATION:
email: wordsavvyhandbook@gmail.com
Twitter: @savvy_be

# Contents

Words Commonly Confused ...................4

Words Commonly Misused .................186

No-No's in Your Speech and Writing....206

Tricky Singulars & Plurals .................215

Words Commonly Misspelled .............227

Answers ....................................239

Author's Note ...........................283

Index ......................................285

# Words Commonly Confused

Who's/Whose on First?

# Master 78 Pairs of Words Most People Confuse

This chapter is designed as a quick, easy-to-use reference for choosing the right word from two (and sometimes three) words commonly confused. For example: "Do I want *accept or except?* ... *farther* or *further?* ... *insure, ensure,* or *assure?*"

There's no need to check the Internet. All the information you need to make a decision is here, available at a glance. In this chapter each pair or trio of commonly confused words is a separate entry, alphabetized and cross-referenced so you can easily find what you want. In addition. memory boosts and a self-quiz are given for each entry to help you remember which word was which.

Entries are set up like this:

 **(1) Quotes** that illustrate use of the entry words by celebrities and well-known public figures. Authors of the quotes encompass a wide range of personages, from Mae West to Winston Churchill to William Shakespeare.

 **(2) Definitions.** Dictionary definitions of the words in question follow the example quotes. Some words have a number of definitions. Not all of these are listed. The most common meanings are, however, along with the word's part of speech.

*Example sentences* are given for the dictionary definitions of a word to illustrate the word's various meanings.

*Usage Notes* are included when needed to explain a common problem in a word's usage or an exception to a usage rule.

**(3) Memory Tricks.** Once you find the right word how can you remember its meaning and how it is distinguished from its confusing partner(s)?

It helps to use "memory tricks." Probably the best aids to memory are those you invent yourself. To help you, however, each entry supplies a few memory boosters, such as mnemonic devices, rhymes, alliterative sentences, connections with related words and spellings, and suggested visualizations.

**(4) Try It.** Each entry ends with a self-quiz to help you see whether or not you understand the material and will apply it when you write. Answers to the quizzes are at the back of the book.

Although the entries provide considerable information to explain "which word is which," providing information is not always enough. Most of -us have had the experience of reading an explanation and thinking that we understand it until we try to apply it. As the saying goes, "The proof is in the pudding." The real test comes when you sit down to write. Will you be on the alert for commonly confused words and remember the distinctions between them? Self-testing helps you see what you have learned and what you only thought you learned.

# ACCEPT ... EXCEPT

## Examples from Quotes

Once we **accept** our limits, we go beyond them.
— *Albert Einstein*

A life isn't significant **except** for its impact on other lives. — *Jackie Robinson*

Everything has been figured out **except** how to live.
— *Jean-Paul Sartre*

## Dictionary Definitions

**accept** *v.* 1. To receive willingly. 2. To agree with; put up with.

I am pleased to *accept* this award.

I *accept* the conclusions of your report.

**except** *prep.* With the exception of; not including. *v.* To exclude; take out from the rest.

Everyone was wrong *except* Harry.

If you *except* weather delays, arrivals were on time.

## Memory Tricks

CONNECT: **accept** → **accept**ance.

VISUALIZE/ALLITERATION: Visualize yourself bowing to thunderous applause after playing an accordion solo. Think, "I gladly **acc**ept your **acc**laim and **acc**olades for my **acc**omplishments on the **acc**ordion."

CONNECT **except** → **except**ion → **except**ional.

VISUALIZE & CONNECT: Visualize yourself beaming and wearing the banner "**Except**ional!" Think, "**Except** for a rare **except**ion, I am **except**ional!"

# Try It!

Choose *accept* or *except* for each ❑.
(See page 239 for answers.)

**1.** It's logical to expect that an Oscar-caliber actor would not ❑ a role in a ridiculously bad movie ❑ under dire circumstances.

**2.** Thus, ❑ for die-hard John Wayne fans, few movie-goers could ❑ Wayne in the incongruous role of Genghis Khan in *The Conqueror.*

**3.** Critics did not ❑ director Dick Powell from responsibility for the absurd Asian Western.

**4.** Evidently Powell was willing to ❑ Wayne's statement that he saw *The Conqueror* as a cowboy film and would play Khan as a gunslinger, ❑ that he slung a sword.

**5.** ❑ for transporting the Gobi Desert to Utah, ❑ for the preposterous casting of the Duke as Genghis Khan and Susan Hayward as a Tartar princess, viewers might have been willing to ❑ the premise of the film.

# ACUTE ... CHRONIC

## Examples from Quotes

I find the pain of a little censure, even when it is unfounded, is more **acute** than the pleasure of much praise. — *Thomas Jefferson*

The shock of any trauma, I think, changes your life. It's more **acute** in the beginning and after a little time you settle back to what you were.
— *Alex Lifeson*

Every citizen who stops smoking, or loses a few pounds, or starts managing his **chronic** disease with real diligence, is caulking a crack for the benefit of us all. — *Mitch Daniels*

## Dictionary Definitions

**acute** *adj.* 1. Sharp; shrewd, keen; penetrating. 2. (Medicine) reaching a crisis rapidly and having a short course (as of a disease).

She has an *acute,* biting wit and always has a ready retort.

He experienced *acute* pain that lasted ten minutes.

**chronic** *adj.* Of long duration; constant.

Pain-relieving medications are only a temporary relief for - *chronic* back pain.

He is, and no doubt will always be, a *chronic* complainer.

# Memory Tricks

CONNECT: **acute** → **cut**. (**Acute** contains the smaller word **cut**. A cut is made by something sharp.)

CONNECT: **acute** → **ac**cident (a critical medical emergency).

CONNECT: **chronic** → **chron**ology. (Both are concerned with a stretch of time. A **chronic** disease is long term. A **chron**ology arranges events in a time sequence.)

 # Try It!

Choose *acute* or *chronic* for each ❑.
(See page 239 for answers.)

**1.** Could the ❑ fatigue I have been plagued with for years be caused by an allergy?

**2.** The dog's ❑ sense of smell quickly picked up the suspect's trail through the woods.

**3.** Your ❑ lateness will get you fired!

**4.** She was immediately sent to the hospital for an ❑ attach of appendicitis.

**5.** Gifted with ❑ intelligence, the chimp easily won the game of checkers from his partner, whose ❑ hyperactivity interfered with her concentration.

**6.** A broken arm is an example of a medical condition that is ❑. Recurring asthma is ❑.

# ADVICE ... ADVISE

## Examples from Quotes

In giving **advice**, seek to help, not to please, our friend. — *Diogenes*

No enemy is worse than bad **advice**. — *Sophocles*

We are so happy to **advise** others that occasionally we even do it in their interest. — *Jules Renard*

I have found the best way to give **advice** to your children is to find out what they want and then **advise** them to do it. — *Harry S. Truman*

## Dictionary Definitions

**advice** *n.* Recommendation; suggestion; counsel; guidance.

> My *advice* is to follow your dream.
>
> Do you want *advice* on how to succeed?

**advise** *v.* 1. Recommend; give advice to. 2. Inform.

> I *advise* reading Napoleon Hill's book *Think and Grow Rich*.
>
> Please *advise* your clients about the new tax laws.

## Memory Tricks

RHYME: **Advice** can be **nice**, like sugar and **spice**, or can lead you to **vice**, such as gambling with **dice**.

RHYME: Always think **twice** before taking **advice**.

RHYME: Since you are so **wise,** then please **advise**; should I "stick to my guns" or **compromise**?

RHYME: Some **advise** you to **exercise** before you eat when you **arise**.

## Try It!

Choose *advice* or *advise* for each ❑.
(See page 240 for answers.)

**1.** Do you need an expert to ❑ you on how to solve your problem?

**2.** Much ❑ is available on what to do when your dog has a skunk encounter.

**3.** The ❑ given by most dog owners is to saturate your pet in tomato juice; others ❑ using vinegar.

**4.** Both pieces of ❑ simply distract the nose without curing the problem.

**5.** What do veterinarians ❑?

**6.** Their ❑ is to mix the following in an open container: 1 quart of 3% hydrogen peroxide, ¼ cup baking soda, and 1-2 tsps. of mild dishwashing detergent that does not contain ammonia or bleach.

**7.** They ❑ saturating your pet's coat with the mixture, then let it set 5 minutes before rinsing.

**8.** One last piece of ❑ is to not keep the mixture in a closed container because it can explode.

# AFFECT ... EFFECT

## Examples from Quotes

The consequences of an act **affect** the probability of its occurring again. — *B. F. Skinner*

Chocolate causes certain endocrine glands to secrete hormones that **affect** your feelings and behavior by making you happy. — *Elaine Sherman*

The best **effect** of fine persons is felt after we have left their presence. — *Ralph Waldo Emerson*

When did we begin to lose faith in our ability to **effect** change? — *Wynton Marsalis*

## Dictionary Definitions

**affect** *v.* 1. To influence; have an effect on. 2. To pretend; feign. 3. *n.* (in psychology) Feeling; emotion.

> The drought will *affect* farmers adversely.
>
> She likes to *affect* a British accent.
>
> The subject's reaction and *affect* were normal.

**effect** *n.* A result; consequence. *v.* To bring about; cause to pass.

> One *effect* of the drought is increased food prices.
>
> It is hoped that the new drug will *effect* a cure.

# Memory Tricks

ALPHABETICAL & LOGICAL ORDER: When you **_affect_** something, you, - produce an **_effect_** on it.

VISUALIZATION & ALLITERATION: (Visualize yourself contemplating enrolling in an expensive course. "Become a Self-Made Millionaire!") Think, "Can I **aff**irm that this would **affect** my **aff**luence, and can I **aff**ord it?"

# Try It!

Choose *affect* or *effect* for each ❑.
(See page 240 for answers.)

**1.** We are all familiar with the ❑ of biting into a red-hot chili pepper.

**2.** We may ❑ indifference, but our taste buds ❑ a protest to the fiery-hot ❑ of capsaicin, the ingredient that causes red-hots to ❑ us with their built-in fire.

**3.** But that fiery ❑ may ❑ us in beneficial ways.

**4.** New studies point to capsaicin's detrimental ❑ on cancer cells.

**5.** For malignant cells, capsaicin can ❑ a premature "death."

**6.** Capsaicin's fiery ❑ is put to use in a barnacle repellant applied to boats.

**7.** Capsaicin can ❑ and dull the perception of pain, an anesthetic ❑.

15

# AGGRAVATE ... IRRITATE

 ## Examples from Quotes

In desperate straits, the fears of the timid **aggravate** the dangers that imperil the brave. — *Christian Nevell Bovee*

Since grief only **aggravates** your loss, grieve not for what is past. — *Walker Perry*

A sure way to **irritate** people and to put evil thoughts into their heads is to keep them waiting a long time. — *Friedrich Nietzsche*

Look at that married woman — sleepless nights and toilsome days cloud her brow and **irritate** her temper. — *Harriot K. Hunt*

 ## Dictionary Definitions

**aggravate** *v.* To make worse; intensify.

Pollutants can *aggravate* allergy symptoms.

**irritate** *v.* 1. To annoy; exasperate. 2. To inflame.

Bruce likes to *irritate* his little brother.

Some strong detergents can *irritate* the skin. (inflame)

USAGE NOTE: In informal usage, *aggravate* and *irritate* are synonyms. In formal usage, the verb *aggravate* means to make worse or more severe, to intensify or make more offensive; whereas the verb

16

*irritate* means to annoy, to provoke anger, or to provoke impatience.

 ## Memory Tricks

CONTRAST: Things are **aggravating**. People are <u>not</u> **aggravated** or **aggravating**. People are **irritated** or **irritating**. (NOTE: This distinction is often ignored in informal usage.)

CONNECT: **aggravate** → make more serious, **grave**.

ALLITERATION: Think, "**Irritating Ir**ving **ir**ks me" (to connect **irritate** with a person).

 ## Try It!

Choose *aggravate* or *irritate* for each ❑.
(See page 241 for answers.)

**1.** Did Jean's remarks ❑ John?

**2.** Did John's temper tantrum ❑ a bad situation?

**3.** Poison ivy can ❑ the skin.

**4.** Can unusual stress ❑ acne?

**5.** Neglect of agriculture can ❑ poverty.

**6.** Little things do not seem to ❑ him.

**7.** Be careful not to ❑ your back pain by lifting those heavy boxes.

**8.** Is he simply in a bad mood, or have I done something to ❑ him?

17

# ALIBI ... EXCUSE

 ## Examples from Quotes

I think the evidence is going to be very clear that he has an absolutely rock-solid **alibi.** — *Bill Thomas*

Never ask a man where he's been. If he's out on legitimate business, he doesn't need an **alibi.**
— *Mae West*

Good taste is the **excuse** I've always given for leading such a bad life. — *Oscar Wilde*

Ambition is a poor **excuse** for not having sense enough to be lazy. — *Charlie McCarthy*

 ## Dictionary Definitions

**alibi** *n.* A defense plea of having been elsewhere when an act was committed.

Since he was in jail at the time of the burglary, he has a cast-iron *alibi.*

**excuse** *n.* An explanation or reason for a failure or shortcoming.

Emerson said that beauty is its own *excuse* for being.

 ## Memory Tricks

CONNECT: **excuse** to the common saying, "*What's your* **excuse**?"

18

ETYMOLOGY: The word *alibi* comes from a Latin word meaning "elsewhere." Legally, you do not have an *alibi* unless you were elsewhere. To remember this, CONNECT **al̲ibi** with **a̲l̲ien**. An alien comes from elsewhere.

## Try It

Choose *alibi* or *excuse* for each ☐.
(See page 241 for answers.)

**1.** He found himself trying to find an ☐ to believe the lie she had told him.

**2.** Do you have an ☐ for the time of the crime?

**3.** In case he got caught, Higgins tried to think of a believable ☐ for why he stashed a change of clothes and false mustache in his car trunk.

**4.** What ☐ did Higgins concoct to convince others he was elsewhere at the time of the crime?

**5.** What was his ☐ for giving false information to the F.B.I about his whereabouts?

**6.** The F.B.I. immediately dismissed Higgins's ☐ that he gave them a false ☐ because he was too embarrassed to admit the truth.

**7.** Although not having an ☐ for the time of a crime is not illegal, it isn't nice to lie to the F.B.I.

19

# ALL READY ... ALREADY

## Examples from Quotes

I'm **all ready** you see. Now my troubles are going to have trouble with me!
—Theodor Seuss Geisel (Dr. Seuss)

We're **all ready** to play and get out there and get it done. — *Dustie Robertson*

There cannot be a crisis today; my schedule is **already** full. —*Henry Kissinger*

Unless you try to do something beyond what you have **already** mastered, you will never grow.
—Ralph Waldo Emerson

## Dictionary Definitions

**all ready** *adj*. Completely ready; prepared.

My bags are packed; I'm **all ready** to go.

**already** *adv*. Prior to; previously; beforehand.

I've **already** packed my bags; I'm ready to go.

## Memory Tricks

LISTEN: Mentally say the sentence you are about to write. If you pause between ***all*** and ***ready***, use two words, **all ready**.

CONNECT: (Visualize runners ready to start a race.) Think, "**All ready**? All set? Go!"

VISUALIZE & CONNECT: Visualize yourself waiting for a friend and looking at your watch, distressed. Think, "It's **al**most 8:00 and we're **already** late!"

## Try It!

Choose *all ready* or *already* for each ☐.
(See page 242 for answers.)

1. Are you ☐ for the big one—an event bigger than the predicted big earthquake in California?

2. This is something that ☐ occurred before, some 65 million years ago, when the Earth was ☐ into the Age of Dinosaurs.

3. An asteroid collided with Earth, producing a dust cloud and resulting cold temperatures that killed thousands of species—and, we are ☐ overdue for another such collision.

4. Preparations have ☐ started to ensure we will be ☐ to prevent our extinction when the next one arrives.

5. We ☐ scan the skies for asteroids.

6. We are making plans so that we will be ☐ to divert asteroids with missiles.

7. Preparations are ☐ being made to avoid a collision so that we will be ☐ for it.

# ALL TOGETHER ... ALTOGETHER

 ## Examples from Quotes

For years, I've pushed the idea of a column compilation book mainly because it would be easy. I could just staple 'em **all together**.
.— *Michael Musto*

Italy and the spring and first love **all together** should suffice to make the gloomiest person happy.
— *Bertrand Russell*

No man who has once heartily and wholly laughed can be **altogether** irreclaimably bad.
— *Thomas Carlyle*

Frankly, I'd like to see the government get out of war **altogether** and leave the whole field to private industry. — *Joseph Heller*

 ## Dictionary Definitions

**all together** *adv.* All at the same time; all at the same place.

> The clothes were thrown *all together* in a heap.

> Let's give a cheer *all together*.

**altogether** *adv.* 1. Entirely. 2. In all.

> I am not *altogether* satisfied with your explanation.

> Volunteers for the mission totaled 63 *altogether*.

> The stream bed dried up *altogether* during the drought.

# Memory Tricks

LISTEN: Mentally say the sentence you are about to write. If you pause between **all** and **together**, use two words, **all together**.

VISUALIZE & CONNECT: Visualize yourself as an elementary school teacher counting your children on a class trip. Think, "Are we **all together?** There should be 20 of us **altogether**."

# Try It!

Choose *all together* or *altogether* for each ❑.
(See page 242 for answers.)

**1.** Are you ❑ positive that Henry is missing?

**2.** We did not stay ❑ as a group all the time.

**3.** I am ❑ certain Henry was with us when we left.

**4.** I distinctly remember us being ❑ on the dock.

**5.** I think we were ❑ when we boarded the ship, but I am not ❑ positive.

**6.** We were not ❑ at the lifeboat drill, and I am sure I did not see Henry there.

**7.** We went to his room ❑, but we found it empty..

**8** Henry is ❑ besotted with Alexandra, but had he stayed behind to be with her or been abducted?

# A LOT (*Not* ALOT) ... ALLOT-

 **Examples from Quotes+**

The reason **a lot** of people do not recognize opportunity is because it usually goes around wearing overalls looking like hard work.
— *Thomas A. Edison*

I really had **a lot** of dreams when I was a kid, and I think a great deal of that grew out of the fact that I had a chance to read **a lot**. — *Bill Gates*

A little talent can create **a lot** of creativity.
— *Richie Norton*

See how the Fates their gifts **allot**. For A is happy, B is not. — *W.S. Gilbert*

Justice is the constant and perpetual will to **allot** to every man his due. — *Domitus Ulpian*

 **Definition Definitions**

**a lot** *n.* A large number or amount. *adv.* To a great degree or extent.

> *A lot* of people write the words "a lot" incorrectly as one word, "a lot."

> His spelling has improved *a lot* this year.

**allot** *v.* 1. To distribute by lot. 2. To allocate.

> How many acres would the government *allot* to a homesteader?

Do you regularly *allot* a portion of your paycheck to your retirement fund?

USAGE NOTE: Although *a lot* is often run together as one word in speaking, it is always incorrect to write it as one word. There is no such word as *alot*.

 ## Memory Tricks

REPEAT ALOUD: ***A*** space ***lot***. ***A*** space ***lot***. Always put a space between ***a*** and ***lot***.

VISUALIZE: Picture yourself splitting a log with an axe and then splitting ***alot*** with an axe into two separate words, ***a lot***. Think, "Split ***a log***, split ***a lot***."

CONNECT: **allot** → **allot**ment

 ## Try It!

Choose *a lot* or *allot* for each ❑.
(See page 243 for answers.)

**1.** If you ❑ time for regular exercise, you will no doubt feel ❑ better.

**2.** Work becomes ❑ easier when you ❑ some of it to others.

**3.** ❑ of people manage to talk ❑ without saying much of anything.

**4.** If you ❑ an acre for corn, you will still have ❑ of acreage for other crops.

25

# AMONG ... BETWEEN

## Examples from Quotes

Liberty cannot be preserved without general knowledge **among** the people. — *John Adams*

**Among** golfers, the putter is usually known as the payoff club, and how right that is! — *Bobby Locke*

Whenever I'm caught **between** two evils, I take the one I've never tried. — *Mae West*

There is so little difference **between** husbands you might as well keep the first.
— *Adela Rogers St. Johns*

## Dictionary Definitions

**among** *prep.* In the midst of; in the company of.

Relax, you're *among* friends.

One of my favorite Agatha Christie mysteries is *Cat* Among *the Pigeons.*

**between** *prep.* 1. In the time or space that separates two individuals or items. 2. Through the combined actions or efforts of both.

A stream runs *between* the two properties.

*Between* us, we have enough money to rent a boat.

Usage Note: The distinction between *among* and *between* lies in number. *Among* applies to a group of three or more. *Between* is used when speaking of two individuals or items. Sometimes, logic supersedes number, however, as explained below.

<u>LOGICAL EXCEPTIONS</u>: Sometimes in a group of items, relationships are considered one-at-a-time *between* one item and each of the others. For example: "I am deciding *between* Tom, Dick, and Harry for the job." In such a case, it would be illogical to use *among*, and *between* is the logical choice.

| Illogical | Logical |
|---|---|
| My choice is *among* vanilla, pistachio, and chocolate. | My choice is *between* vanilla, pistachio, and chocolate. |
| There are few houses *among* the three lakes. | There are few houses *between* the three lakes. |
| She was deciding *among* Princeton, Yale, and Harvard. | She was deciding *between* Princeton, Yale, and Harvard. |

 **Memory Tricks**

CONNECT: Connect the **tw** in **be<u>tw</u>een** with "**two** words": **two**, **tw**in, **tw**enty, **tw**ain, **tw**ice.

CONNECT: ***among*** → "honor ***among*** thieves," "rose ***among*** the thorns;" "cat ***among*** the pigeons."

# Try It!

Choose *among* or *between* for each ☐.
(See page 243 for answers.)

**1.** The nearest pharmacy is ☐ the grocery store and the pet store.

**2.** We divided the reward money ☐ the three of us.

**3.** Warning! ☐ the beautiful flowers in our gardens are four that can be deadly.

**4.** Is that foxglove ☐ the two rosebushes?

**5.** Careful—its flowers are ☐ the most poisonous if you eat them.

**6.** The charming autumn crocus is ☐ the few flowers that bloom before they have leaves.

**7.** But autumn crocus flowers are poisonous and have caused several deaths ☐ those who found them in the woods and tried to eat them.

**8.** The beautiful flowers of oleander and angel's trumpet are ☐ the garden's most deadly.

**9.** ☐ the beauties of the garden lie some hazards, but only if you eat the flowers.

## AS *See* LIKE

## AS IF *See* LIKE

# ASSURE ... ENSURE ... INSURE

 ## Examples from Quotes

Some people think football is a matter of life and death. I **assure** you, it's much more serious than that. — *Bill Shankly*

Students rarely disappoint teachers who **assure** them in advance that they are doomed to failure. — *Sidney Hook*

One should always **ensure** a clean environment while making food. — *Rig Veda*

**Ensure** that your script is watertight. If it's not on the page, it will never magically appear on the screen. — *Richard E. Grant*

You know, my dear, I **insured** my voice for fifty thousand dollars. — *Miriam Hopkins*

We can never **insure** 100 percent of the population against 100 percent of the hazards and vicissitudes of life. — *Franklin D. Roosevelt*

 ## Dictionary Definitions

**assure** *v.* 1. To impart certainty. 2. To reassure or guarantee, often through words or gestures.

Your check is in the mail, I *assure* you.

**ensure** *v.* To make safe or certain, often by taking some action.

Make a reservation to *ensure* you get on that flight.

**insure** *v.* To provide or buy insurance for, usually to obtain financial security.

Does your policy *insure* you against flood damage?

 ## Memory Tricks

CONNECT: **assure** → re**assure**. (You **assure** and re**assure** people, not things.)

VISUALIZE & CONNECT: (Visualize yourself putting a check made out to "**EN**" in an **en**velope.) Think: "**En**close the check in an **en**velope to **en**sure payment."

CONNECT: **insure** → life **insur**ance.

## Try It!

Choose *assure, ensure,* or *insure* for each ❑. (See page 244 for answers.)

**1.** Do you need to ❑ the contents of this package?

**2.** Send your letter by Priority Mail to ❑ that it arrives by Friday.

**3.** Let me ❑ you that I will ❑ the vase against loss, and I will double-box it to ❑ its safe delivery.

**4.** Be sure to ❑ students that our correspondence course will help ❑ their success in picking the right stocks.

**5.** Did you ❑ your house for its replacement value?

# A WHILE ... AWHILE

## Examples from Quotes

Every once in **a while**, you let a word or phrase out and you want to catch it and bring it back.
— *Dan Quayle*

It took me **a while** to realize that basketball isn't football. — *Merlin Olsen*

I think I'm going to be around **awhile**.
— *Dan Merino*

Never be afraid to sit **awhile** and think.
— *Lorraine Hansberry*

## Dictionary Definitions

**a while** *article + n.* A short period of time.

It has been *a while* since I've played golf.

Let's stop and rest for *a while*.

**awhile** *adv.* For a short period of time.

Let's stop and rest awhile.

I lived *awhile* in New York before I moved to Hoboken.

USAGE NOTE: The common mistake is to write *awhile* instead of *a while*. This is such a common error that even printed quotations show an incorrect usage: *awhile* instead of the correct *a while*. Think of *awhile* as three words contracted into one: *for a while* = *awhile*. Only write

31

the single word *awhile* when you mean "for a while." Likewise, never write *for awhile*. That is redundant because "for" is included in the meaning of *awhile*.

## Memory Trick

LAW OF AVERAGES: In most cases, it is correct to write the separate words **a while**. (It is even correct to write "for a while" (but not *"for awhile"*).

## Try It!

Choose *a while* or *awhile* for each ☐
(See page 244 for answers.)

**1.** The plan is to continue working ☐ and then break for lunch.

**2.** Once in ☐ I think of Cape Cod and begrudge the fact that it has been ☐ since I've been able to take a vacation.

**3.** I would love to sit ☐ and watch the sun set on Cape Cod Bay.

**4.** Since it may take ☐ to catch a fish, let's plan on being here for ☐.

**5.** We'll fish ☐, and in ☐ we'll head for shore.

**6.** Will you think of me once in ☐?

**7.** Children, please sit down and be quiet for ☐.

# BAD ... BADLY

 **Examples from Quotes**

There is nothing so **bad** or so good that you will not find an Englishman doing it.
—*George Bernard Shaw*

Growing old is nothing more than a **bad** habit which a busy man has no time to form.
—André Maurois

It is less dangerous to treat most men **badly** than to treat them too well. —*Francois La Rochefoucauld*

To withhold deserved praise lest it should make its object conceited is as dishonest as to withhold payment of a debt lest your creditor should spend the money **badly**. —*George Bernard Shaw*

 **Dictionary Definitions**

**bad** *adj.* 1. Inferior; unacceptable. 2. Evil; wicked. 3. Naughty; mischievous. 4. Unpleasant; disagreeable. 5. Unfavorable. 6. Rotten; spoiled. 7. Injurious; harmful. 8. Invalid. 9. Regretful; sorry.

Put that coat down, Fang! *Bad* dog!

Fang, you have earned your *bad* reputation. That raccoon coat smells *bad*. (It "stinks.")

33

**badly** *adv.* In a bad manner.  2. Greatly. Very much.

> Fang's no bloodhound; he smells *badly*. (His sense of smell is faulty.)
>
> Fang responds *badly* to criticism.
>
> That roof needs repair *badly*.

USAGE NOTES: A linking verb (*is, feels, looks, tastes, smells, seems*) is followed by an adjective or noun. *Bad* used as an adjective or a noun can follow a linking verb.

<u>CORRECT</u>: I feel *bad*.

<u>INCORRECT</u>: I feel *badly*.

*Badly* is an adverb used with action verbs, not linking verbs.

<u>CORRECT</u>: The team <u>played</u> *badly*

<u>INCORRECT</u>: The team played *bad*

 **Memory Tricks**

GRAMMAR: The ending *–ly* is an adverb ending. **Badly** is an adverb that tells "how" about a verb. Played how? Played *badly*.

CONTRAST/CONNECT: Contrast **good** with **bad.**

CONTRAST AND CONNECT:  **good** dog →**bad** dog.

RHYME: **Sadly**, you play **badly**.

## *Try* It!

Choose *bad* or *badly* for each ☐.
(See page 244 for answers.)

**1**. The musicians performed ☐ at rehearsal.

**2**. She felt ☐ about her mistake.

**3**. He was ☐ scarred after a ☐ encounter with a grizzly bear.

**4**. Mandrake was an evil tyrant, ☐ from birth, who treated his subjects ☐.

**5**. I was ☐ distressed on learning that he had paid me with a ☐ check.

**6**. The audience responded ☐ to the tenor's outrageously ☐ rendition of "Oh, Sole Mio" and began pelting the stage with rotten bananas and ☐ tomatoes.

## BETWEEN *See* AMONG

# BRAKE ... BREAK

## Examples from Quotes

When you step on the **brakes**, your life is in your
`foot's hand. — *George Carlin*

Living with a conscience is like driving a car with
the **brakes** on. — *Budd Schulberg*

What **breaks** in a moment may take years to mend.
— Swedish proverb

Take the rope apart, separate it into the smallest
threads that compose it, and you can **break** them
one by one. — *Victor Hugo*

## Dictionary Definitions

**brake** *n.* A device to slow down or stop something.
*v.* The action of applying such a device.

He slammed on the car's *brakes* to avoid hitting the deer.

He was able to *brake* in time to avoid a collision.

**break** *v.* 1. To smash or shatter. 2. To separate
into parts by force. 3. To take an intermission. 4.
To violate a rule. *n.* 1. The act or result of breaking.
2. An opening or beginning. 3. An interruption
from work. 4. A chance occurrence.

Fortunately, the vase did not *break* when I dropped it.

*Break* two eggs into the frying pan.

The dance band took a ten-minute *break.*

If you *break* the curfew, you will pay a fine.

Winning the lottery was a lucky *break*.

## Memory Tricks

RHYME: Don't **quake, Jake**. Hit the **brake**!

CONNECT: **break** → **break***fast*. When you have **break***fast*, you **break** your overnight fast.

## Try It!

Choose *brake(s)* or *break(s)* for each ❑.
(See page 245 for answers.)

**1.** When you want to wish an actor good luck you say, "❑ a leg!"

**2.** Don't step on the ❑ pedal when you're on a patch of ice.

**3.** The team got the ❑ they needed to ❑ their losing streak.

**4.** The car's ❑ fluid leaked out because of a ❑ in its ❑ hose, and the ❑ wouldn't work.

**5.** In a truck or train, pressurized air, not fluid, is used to put on the ❑.

**6.** Josh has never been known to ❑ a rule.

# BRING ... TAKE

## Examples from Quotes

The person who can **bring** the spirit of laughter into a room is indeed blessed. — *Bennett Cerf*

I **bring** to my life a certain amount of mess. — Kitty O'Neill Collins

**Take** my wife . . . Please! — *Henny Youngman*

It is better to **take** what does not belong to you than to let it lie around neglected. — *Mark Twain*

## Dictionary Definitions

**bring** *v.* To convey or escort with oneself to a place.

Shall I *bring* my guitar when I visit you?

**take** *v.* To carry or cause to go along with oneself to another place.

Please *take* your dog home now.

You may *take* our plates and *bring* the check now.

USAGE NOTE: *Bring* indicates conveyance toward the speaker. (*Bring* it here = Come here with that.) *Take* indicates conveyance to a place away from the speaker. (*Take* that away = Take that away from here with you.)

# Memory Tricks

VISUALIZE & RHYME: Visualize a groom asking his best man, "Did you **bring** the **ring**?"

VISUALIZE: Visualize a plane **taking** off. It moves away from you.

# Try It!

Choose *bring* or *take* for each ☐.
(See page 245 for answers.)

1. ☐ this to the bank and ☐ back a receipt.

2. In the 1920s, Charles Ponzi promised to ☐ investors a 100% return in 30 days.

3. Thousands of greedy, gullible investors were only too happy to ☐ their money to Ponzi.

4. They thought he would ☐ it to invest.

5. In reality, he used it to pay former investors, who expected him to ☐ them a "return."

6. It was inevitable that the scheme would one day collapse and ☐ the authorities to Ponzi's door.

7. Ponzi's schemes were destined to first ☐ him away to court, and from there, ☐ him to the hoosegow.

8. Ponzi's stint in the cooler did not ☐ Ponzi lasting disgrace, for he later landed a job with Alitalia Airlines.

39

# CAN ... MAY

## Examples from Quotes

My fellow Americans, ask not what your country **can** do for you, ask what you **can** do for your country. — *John F. Kennedy*

You **can** always count on Americans to do the right thing—after they've tried everything else.
— *Winston Churchill*

**May** I try some of your tasty beverages?
— *Samuel L. Jackson*

**May** I kiss you then? On this miserable paper? I might as well open the window and kiss the night air. — *Franz Kafka*

**can** *aux. v.* (formal) Be able.

The drummer *can* read music.

She *can* prove she's right.

**may** *aux. v.* Have permission.

*May* I use the red Jaguar tonight?

You *may* not step on my white carpet with muddy boots!

USAGE NOTE: Both *can* and *may* have additional meanings, but in formal usage, the above meanings are those that are confused. In informal writing, *can* and *may* are used interchangeably to indicate permission.

**Memory Tricks**

CONNECT **can** with the book *The Little Engine That Could.* As the little engine strains to go up the hill, it chants: "I think I **can**, I think I **can**, I think I **can**." (Not: "I think I *may,* I think I *may,* I think I *may.*")

CONNECT CAN → **can** do, meaning "be able to."

CONNECT: **may** with asking permission in the song "Mother, **May** I Go Out to Swim?"

RHYME: **May** I kiss you, yea or **nay**?

 **Try It!**

Choose *can* ("be able") or *may* ("have permission") for each ☐. (See page 245 for answers.)

**1.** You ☐ come into my garden to look at the flowers, but beware!

**2**. The beautiful foxglove flowers are poisonous. They ☐ kill you

**3** You ☐ look, touch, and smell. But don't eat them unless you ☐ withstand the stress and discomfort of a wildly racing heart.

**4.** On the other hand, foxglove is the source of digitalis, which ☐ strengthen the heart.

# CAPITAL ... CAPITOL

 ## Examples from Quotes

Memphis is the blues **capital** of the world, we like to say. — *Justin Timberlake*

The highest use of **capital** is not to make more money, but to make money do more for the betterment of life. — *Henry Ford*

We knew there were a few unidentified planes that may have been headed for the White House or the **Capitol** building. — *Mercer Reynolds*

 ## Dictionary Definitions

**capital** *n.* 1. A city that is the seat of a state or national government. 2. Money or real estate used to produce more wealth. 3. A letter of the alphabet written larger size or printed in upper-case type.

Washington, D.C., the *capital* of the United States, was founded in 1790.

Part of the corporation's *capital* is in the form of real estate.

The first word of a sentence begins with a *capital* letter.

**capitol** *n.* The building where a state legislature meets.

Tennessee's *capitol* building sits on a hill overlooking Nashville.

**Capitol** n. The building in Washington, D.C., where the Congress of the United States assembles.

> The cast-iron dome of the United States *Capitol* is a famous American landmark.

## Memory Tricks

SIMPLIFY: You can't go wrong if you remember that **capitol** is a building. because that is its only meaning. All other meanings have an *al* ending.

VISUALIZE: To remember which word names a building, picture the famous dome of the U.S. Capitol in Washington, D.C. Its shape is similar to the letter **O**, and the words *dome* and **capitol** have an *o* in them.

## Try It!

Choose *capital, capitol,* or *Capitol.* for each ☐.
(See page 246 for answers.)

**1.** What is the ☐ of New Jersey?

**2.** The state ☐ is made of granite.

**3.** Proposed changes to the ☐ gains tax are under discussion on ☐ Hill in the nation's ☐.

**4.** Should the name of a pet begin with a ☐ letter?

**5**. Each state ☐ has a ☐ building where its legislature meets.

# CENSOR ... CENSURE

## Examples from Quotes

> One of my concerns is that writers will begin to feel the **censor** on their backs, and we won't get their very best. — *Judy Blume*

> No government ought to be without **censors**, and where the press is free no one ever will.
> — Thomas Jefferson

> **Censure** is the tax a man pays to the public for being eminent. — *Jonathan Swift*

> You do ill if you praise but worse if you **censure** what you do not understand. — *Leonardo da Vinci*

## Dictionary Definitions

**censor** *n.* An official examiner who scrutinizes multimedia materials for objectionable content. *v.* To examine multimedia materials for any objectionable content.

> The *censor* checked the script to be sure it was suitable for family TV.

> He decided to *censor* her speech before reading it aloud.

**censure** *n.* An expression of criticism, blame, or disapproval. *v.* To express blame or disapproval.

> The senator knew she would face the *censure* of her colleagues for opposing them and voting "Yes."

The judge was quick to *censure* the defendant's outrageous courtroom behavior.

 ## Memory Tricks

VISUALIZE & CONNECT: **censor** → **Oh**, my! (Visualize a **censor** looking at the pages of a book in shocked horror and saying, "**O**h, my!")

CONNECT: **censor** → **censor**ship.

CONNECT: **censure** → **ju**dge and the letter **u**. Think, "The **ju**dge is s**u**re to **cens**u**re** and reb**u**ke r**u**de remarks."

## Try It!

Choose *censor* or *censure* for each ☐
(See page 246 for answers.)

**1.** The TV ☐ deleted a segment from the sitcom.

**2.** During the war, a ☐ checked soldiers' outgoing letters for information of benefit to the enemy.

**3.** It is unusual for such a prominent politician to escape criticism and ☐.

**4.** According to Demosthenes, the most effective way to get rid of ☐ is to correct ourselves.

**5.** What do you think Juvenal meant when he said that ☐ acquits the raven, but pursues the dove?

**6.** Please ☐ your outrageous, offensive remarks in front of the children!

**7.** According to one newscaster, twenty-two percent of the people in the United States believe that the government should ☐ newspapers.

**8.** Do you agree with William Gilmore Simms that the dread of ☐ is the death of genius?

**9.** The rude remark had left my lips before I was able to ☐ it.

**10.** He felt an uncontrollable need to ☐ others, to express his extreme disapproval.

**11.** You need to ☐ some of your content if you are intending to publish your book for children.

**12.** As soon as the letter had been sent, I wanted to ☐ it, to call it back, to change my wording.

**13.** The only thing that holds his bad behavior in check is his fear of ☐.

**14.** The ☐ struck out two scenes from the film.

# CHORD ... CORD

## Examples from Quotes

When you have 13 horns, and one is soloing, you have 12 people to play the richest, fullest **chord** you could ever imagine behind that solo. — *Carla Bley*

Every action in our lives touches on some **chord** that will vibrate in eternity.
— Edwin Hubbel Chapin

No **cord** or cable can draw so forcibly, or bind so fast, as love can do with a single thread.
— Robert Burton

For people who like peace and quiet: a phoneless **cord.** — *Unknown*

## Dictionary Definitions

**chord** *n.* 1. Three or more musical tones sounded simultaneously. 2. An emotional response.

The song ended as it began, with a C-minor *chord*.

Her kind words struck a sympathetic *chord*.

**cord** *n.* 1. A string or cable. 2. A ropelike anatomical structure. 3. A unit of cut wood.

Tie the package carefully with strong *cord*.

Don't strain your vocal *cords*.

We need to buy a *cord* of firewood.

# Memory Tricks

CONNECT: **chord** → **chorus** → **choral**. (If its meaning is musical, the word is **chord** with an **h**.)

VISUALIZE & RHYME: A **cord** is wrapped around a **Ford**. Cut the **cord** with a **sword**.

# Try It!

Choose *chord* of *cord* for each ◻.
(See page 247 for answers.)

**1.** Do you have a ◻ long enough go around a ◻ of wood, which is 4 by 4 by 8 feet?

**2.** The sonata's opening ◻ progression set a plaintive note that struck a responsive ◻ in the audience.

**3.** Fortunately, his spinal ◻ was not injured when a ◻ of wood fell off the truck on top of him.

**4.** His unfortunate demonstration of the fire hazards of overloading an electrical outlet struck a ◻ of alarm in the audience.

**5.** The demonstration—which consisted of plugging in a power ◻ from a space heater plus an extension ◻ to which was attached the electric ◻ to a toaster and the ◻ to a hair-dryer—proved the old adage about where there's smoke, there's fire!

## CHRONIC *See* ACUTE

# CITE ... SIGHT ... SITE

 **Examples from Quotes**

The devil can **cite** Scripture for his purpose.
— *William Shakespeare*

Those who have heard me speak from time to time know that quite often I **cite** the observation of that great American author, Mark Twain, who said, history does not repeat itself, but it rhymes.
— *J. D. Hayworth*

After marriage, a woman's **sight** becomes so keen that she can see right through her husband without looking at him, and a man's so dull that he can look right through his wife without seeing her.
— Helen Rowland

He fell in love with himself at first **sight**, and it is a passion to which he has always remained faithful.
— Anthony Powell

An architect's most useful tools are an eraser at the drawing board and a wrecking bar at the **site**.
— *Frank Lloyd Wright*

Blogs are a great way to monitor and even participate in the chatter about your new **site**.
— *Mike Davidson*

# Dictionary Definitions

**cite** *v.* 1. To quote as an example, authority, or proof. 2. To summon before a court.

> She found it embarrassing for her teacher to *cite* her as a good example.
>
> Will the officer *cite* me for speeding?
>
> Be sure to *cite* the source of facts in your paper.

**sight** *n.* 1. The ability to see. 2. Something that is seen.

> His *sight* was impaired by the heavy smoke.
>
> Is any *sight* more welcome than a baby's smile?

**site** *n.* The place where something is, was, or will be located.

> I think I dropped my wallet at the construction *site*.
>
> I am having some difficulty designing my own Web *site*.

 # Memory Tricks

CONNECT: **cite** → **cit**ation.

CONNECT: **sight** →**sight**seeing.

CONNECT: **site** → **sit**uated.

# Try It!

Choose *cite, sight,* or *site* for each ☐.
(See page 247 for answers.)

**1.** We're standing on the ☐ of the first schoolhouse in Tennessee.

**2.** What a ☐ to be on the ☐ at Cape Canaveral when a space shuttle is launched!

**3.** To ☐ the sentiments of George Bernard Shaw, "Beauty is all very well at first ☐; but who ever looks at it when it has been in the house for three days?"

**4.** Can you ☐ an example of a Web ☐ that gives information on the senses of hearing and ☐ of the various reptiles?

**5.** Go to NASCAR.com, the official ☐ of NASCAR, to see dramatic shots of the Bristol Motor Speedway, an amazing ☐ for the eyes, which many ☐ as the "Coliseum of Confusion."

**6.** To ☐ the words of racing legend Mario Andretti, "Circumstances may cause interruptions and delays, but never lose ☐ of your goal."

**7.** Can you ☐ a few examples in support of your argument?

**8.** We need to be cautious and stay out of ☐.

# COARSE ... COURSE

 **Examples from Quotes**

For the first time, the weird and the stupid and the **coarse** are becoming our cultural norms, even our cultural ideal. — *Carl Bernstein*

The bosom can ache beneath diamond brooches; and many a blithe heart dances under **coarse** wool. — *Edwin Hubbel Chapin*

You don't change the **course** of history by turning the faces of portraits to the wall. — *Jawaharial Nehru*

A golf **cours**e is nothing but a pool room moved outdoors. — *Frank Butler*

I took a speed-reading **cours**e and read *War and Peace* in twenty minutes. It involves Russia. — *Woody Allen*

 **Dictionary Definitions**

**coarse** *adj.* 1. Rough, harsh. 2. Crude, lacking in refinement.

The burlap fabric felt too *coarse* and bristly to be worn against the skin

Of *course*, his *coarse* language and manners will be frowned upon by "polite society."

**course** *n.* 1. A path of progress or action. 2. A route or path. 3. A series of educational materials dealing with a given subject. *v.* To run swiftly or pursue.4. *Of course.* Certainly; as might be expected.

> The race *course* has harness racing from April through November.
>
> How much is the textbook for the humanities *course*?
>
> Blood *courses* swiftly through the blood vessels on its *course* through the body.

 ## Memory Tricks

CONNECT: **a** in *sandpaper* with the **a** in *co**a**rse.* Think: "**S**andpaper feels co**a**rse."

CONNECT: **u** in *run* with the **u** in course. THINK: "Horses r**u**n on a race co**u**rse.
"

 ## Try It!

Choose *coarse* or *course* for each ☐.
(See page 248 for answers.)

**1.** Does the ☐ of true love ever run smooth?

**2.** The film's ☐ language was edited for TV.

**3.** You'll find Harry on the golf ☐₁ of ☐.

**4.** The ☐ is required in order to get your degree.

# 5. OUR SHIP'S ☐ IS SET, AND WE'LL ARRIVE IN DUE ☐.

# COMPARE ... CONTRAST

## Examples from Quotes

Shall I **compare** thee to a summer's day? Thou art more lovely and more temperate.
— *William Shakespeare*

I don't **compare** 'em, I just catch 'em. — *Willie Mays*

In Mozart and Salieri we see the **contrast** between the genius which does what it must and the talent which does what it can. — *Maurice Baring*

A wonderful thing about a book, in **contrast** to a computer screen, is that you can take it to bed with you. — *Daniel J. Boorstin*

## Dictionary Definitions

**compare** *v.* To examine similarities or likenesses.

If you *compare* the two plots, you will find they are remarkably similar.

**contrast** *v.* To show or emphasize differences. *n.* Something that shows a marked difference to something else.

*Contrast* the appearance of the garden in winter and in summer.

Notice the strong *contrast* of light and dark in this photograph.

# Memory Tricks

CONNECT: **compare** → **compar**able.

RHYME: FIRST and **last**, slow and **fast**, present and **past**, small and **vast**. Those are some pairs that make a **contrast.**

# Try It!

Choose *compare* or *contrast* for each ❑.
(See page 248 for answers.)

**1**. Adjust the TV picture so there is less ❑.

**2**. In ❑ to her blonde twin sister, Kim has red hair.

**3**. If you ❑ the two photographs of the oak tree, you'll see that the one on the right has more ❑.

**4.** Obviously, Jack and Jill are not identical twins, but if you ❑ them, you'll find that their facial features are similar.

**5.** If an essay question asks you to ❑ the pre-Civil War economies of the North versus the South, it is asking you to discuss their differences.

**6.** If you ❑ an armadillo to a turtle, you will see that each has a kind of protective armor, or hell."

**7.** But whereas the armadillo is warm-blooded and a mammal, the turtle, in ❑, is cold-blooded and a reptile.

55

# COMPLEMENT ... COMPLIMENT

 **Examples from Quotes**

Guilt always hurries towards its **complement**, punishment; only there does its satisfaction lie. — Lawrence Durrell

I have the normal **complement** of anxieties, neuroses, psychoses and whatever else—but I'm absolutely nothing special. — *Clive Barker*

Whenever a man's friends begin to **compliment** him about looking young, he may be sure that they think he is growing old. — *Victor Hugo*

The greatest **compliment** that was ever paid me was when one asked me what I thought, and attended to my answer. — *Henry David Thoreau*

 **Dictionary Definitions**

**complement** *n.* Something that completes or makes perfect. *v.* To serve as a *complement* to.

This wine is a perfect *complement* to the meal.

You need strappy sandals to *complement* the dress.

**compliment** *n.* An expression of praise, respect, or admiration. *v.* To pay a *compliment* to.

Was his *compliment* genuine or was it flattery?

I'd like to *compliment* you on your beautiful singing.

# Memory Tricks

CONNECT: The **e** in **complement** to the **e** in complete. Think: "A **complement** completes something."

CONNECT: The **i** in **compliment** to the **i** in like and nice. Think: "I like a **compliment**. A **compliment** is nice."

 # Try It!

Choose *complement* or *compliment* for each ☐.
(See page 249 for answers.)

Early in the game, cereal manufacturers learned to use the cereal box to distinguish a product from its competitors and to ☐ its contents. Both celebrities and cartoon characters were paid the ☐ of being a product's mascot. Mascots were chosen to ☐ the product's perceived features. For example, the choice of Norman Rockwell to paint a red-haired, freckle-faced boy for Kellogg's Corn Flakes, was a ☐ to Rockwell's ability to project a homey, family image that would ☐ the message, "Buy Kellogg's Corn Flakes for your kids." Even the box's background color, white, was chosen to ☐ the pure, clean image targeted for the product, just as yellow was chosen as a ☐ for the cheerful, energy-packed image designed for Kellogg's Sugar Corn Pops. For many reasons, high sales of a boxed cereal are a ☐ to its designer's ability to effectively ☐ the product's personality, or image.

# COMPOSE ... COMPRISE

## Examples from Quotes

It is not hard to **compose**, but what is fabulously hard is to leave the superfluous notes under the table. — *Johannes Brahms*

All the choir of heaven and furniture of earth—in a word, all those bodies which **compose** the frame of the world—have not any subsistence without a mind. — *George Berkeley*

Courage is what preserves our liberty, safety, life, and our homes and parents, our country and children. Courage **comprises** all things.
— Titus Maccius Plautus

The Tertiary (surface of the earth's crust **comprises** railway tracks, patent pavements, grass, snakes, moldy boots, beer bottles, tomato cans, intoxicated citizens, garbage, anarchists, snap-dogs, and fools.
— Ambrose Bierce

## Dictionary Definitions

**compose** *v.* 1. To form; to make up the parts of a whole. 2. To create.

What three branches *compose* the federal government?

Some composers use the piano as they ***compose*** music.

**comprise** *v.* To consist of; to contain.

> The property *comprises* three acres of forest and a cranberry bog.
>
> The festival *comprises* events for children and for adults.

USAGE NOTE: Never use <u>*comprised*</u> <u>*of*</u>. *Comprised* means "included;" you wouldn't say "included of."

 ## Memory Tricks

CONTRAST:  The whole **comprises** the parts; parts **compose** the whole.

CONNECT: **compose** → **composer**→ **compos**ition.

RHYME: I **chose** to **compose** an ode to a **rose**.

RHYME: I choose my wardrobe to **comprise** clothes that flatter and **disguise** my **thighs.**

 ## Try It!

Choose *compose* or *comprise* for each ❑.
(See page 249 for answers.)

**1.** Orchestras ❑ four groups of instruments: strings, woodwinds, brass, and percussion.

**2.** She began to ❑ a "Dear John" letter to Harry.

**3.** These books ❑ all that remains of his library.

**4.** Eleven of the finest players ❑ the All-Star Team.

**5.** What four bodies of water ❑ the Great Lakes?

# CONNOTE ... DENOTE

 **Examples from Quotes**

Freedom is not worth having if it does not **connote** freedom to err. — *Mahatma Gandhi*

I always thought that piracy **connotes** something glamorous. Let's call it what it is: theft.
— *Barry M. Meyer*

Though gray be your hair, with little to part, this does not **denote**, the age of your heart
— *Michael Franklin Ellis*

He had that curious love of green, which in individuals is always the sign of a subtle artistic temperament, and in nations is said to **denote** a laxity, if not a decadence of morals.
— *Oscar Wilde*

 **Dictionary Definitions**

**connote** *v.* To imply emotional associations that accompany a literal meaning.

She wrote "home" rather than "house" to *connote* a warm, homey dwelling.

**denote** *v.* To convey a literal, explicit meaning.

Two words can *denote* the same thing, but carry different associations.

The words "clunker" and "Ferrari" both *denote* "car," but have different connotations.

# Memory Tricks

ETYMOLOGY: **Connote** comes from **con-**, meaning "together with," and **note**, meaning "to note or mark." Think, "**Connote** means <u>noting</u> what a word stands for <u>together</u> <u>with</u> its associations."

CONNECT: **<u>d</u>enote** → **<u>d</u>ictionary**. Think, "What a word **denotes** is its literal, or **<u>d</u>ictionary** meaning."

# Try It!

Choose *connote* or *denote* for each ◻.
(See page 250 for answers.)

**1.** What kind of animal does the word *dog* ◻?

**2.** The word *mutt* is a synonym for *dog*, but what negative or positive associations does the word *mutt* ◻?

**3.** Both *skinny* and *svelte* ◻ thinness, but they do not ◻ the same view of that quality.

**4.** Would you choose the word *thrifty* or *miserly* to ◻ a positive view of someone who is careful about spending money?

**5.** A copywriter carefully chooses words that ◻ positive associations.

**6.** That symbol on the sign is used to ◻ danger.

**7.** The perfume's name is meant to ◻ luxury.

61

# CONTINUAL ... CONTINUOUS

## Examples from Quotes

A **continual** atmosphere of hectic passion is very trying if you haven't got any of your own.
— Dorothy L. Sayers

Without **continual** growth and progress, such words as improvement, achievement, and success have no meaning. — *Benjamin Franklin*

**Continuous** effort—not strength or intelligence—is the key to unlocking our potential.
— *Winston Churchill*

View life as a **continuous** learning experience.
— *Denis Waitley*

## Dictionary Definitions

**continual** *adj.* Occurring repeatedly, but with interruptions.

I am tired of your *continual* complaints.

My New Year's resolution is to strive for *continual* improvement.

**continuous** *adj.* Occurring constantly, without interruption.

The *continuous* noise of the fan kept me awake.

The Earth move in a *continuous* journey around the sun.

## Memory Tricks

CONNECT the **a** in **continual** with the **a** in **again**. Something that is **continual** happens **again** and **again**.

CONNECT the **ous** in **continuous** to → **One Unending Sequence**. (Something that is **continuous** is unending.)

CONNECT the **o** in **continuous** with a circle. The letter **o** looks like a circle, and a circle is **continuous**, unending.

## Try It!

Choose *continual* or *continuous* for each ◻. (See page 250 for answers.)

**1.** The ◻ barking of that dog is an annoyance.

**2.** There is a ◻ stream of traffic downtown.

**3.** She listened to the ◻ rush of water over the dam punctuated by a ◻ stop-and-start buzz of a saw.

**4.** The uninterrupted, ◻ loud music from the apartment was a source of constant irritation.

**5.** The speaker droned on interminably in a ◻ monotone in spite of ◻ attempts to cut him off.


## CONTRAST *See* COMPARE
## CORD *See* CHORD

# COUNCIL ... COUNSEL

## Examples from Quotes

Now, I cannot approve anything the **council** has rejected, but I can reject anything the **council** has approved. — *Jane Alexander*

The **council** now beginning rises in the Church like the daybreak, a forerunner of most splendid light. — Pope John XXIII

Who cannot give good **counsel**? 'Tis cheap, it costs them nothing. — *Robert Burton*

It is a light thing for whoever keeps his foot outside trouble to advise and **counsel** him that suffers. — *Aeschylus*

## Dictionary Definitions

**council** *n.* A group of people that meets to discuss and develop policy.

The safety *council* meets once a month.

**counsel** *n.* 1. A discussion; a consultation. 2. Advice. 3. A lawyer or lawyers. *v.* To offer advice.

They held a *counsel* to discuss their alternatives.

I will follow my doctor's *counsel* to stop smoking.

The *counsel* for the defense questioned the first witness.

Parents *counsel* their children.

## Memory Tricks

CONNECT the *il* in **council** with "group of people."
Think: "*Bill, Phil, Jill,* and *Will* are in the town **council**."

CONNECT the *el* in **counsel** with the *el* in *help*.
(**Counsel** is h*el*p, or advice.)

## Try It!

Choose *council* or *counsel* for each ☐.
(See page 250 for answers.)

**1.** When O'Reilly was in high school, he was elected to the student ☐.

**2.** Let's hold a ☐ to decide how to present our plan to city ☐.

**3.** I am seeking your ☐ on how to find a ☐ for the defense.

**4.** Her ☐ was that it was advisable to seek the ☐ of an attorney who has expertise in such matters.

**5.** On advice of ☐, the ☐ decided not to allocate any more funds for the questionable project.

**6.** Her ☐ advised her that she should first seek ☐ from an expert and then approach the town ☐.

## COURSE *See* COARSE

## DENOTE *See* CONNOTE

65

# DESERT ... DESSERT

 **Examples from Quotes**

All sunshine makes a **desert**. —Arabic Proverb

People in my books tend to get their just **deserts**, even if not at the hands of the police.
—Antonia Fraser

Being a good psychoanalyst, in short, has the same disadvantage as being a good parent. The children **desert** one as they grow up. — Morton Hunt

Drama is like a plate of meat and potatoes, comedy is rather the **dessert**, a bit like meringue.
— *Woody Allen*

 **Dictionary Definitions**

**desert** *n.* 1, An arid, barren land. 2. (*usually plural*) Deserved punishment or reward (e.g., "just deserts"). *v.* To abandon.

This *desert* receives less than ten inches of rain annually.

You will receive your just *deserts* for spreading those malicious lies.

I cannot *desert* you in your hour of need.

**dessert** *n.* A sweet treat, usually served at the end of a meal.

My favorite *dessert*? It's a toss-up between tiramisu and pecan pie.

# Memory Tricks

SIMPLIFY: **Dessert**, with a double **s**, has only one meaning: "The sweet treat you eat at the end of the meal." This simplifies matters, since every other meaning is spelled with one **s**, **desert**.

CONNECT: To remember which word in the pair has a double **s**, think: "A **dessert** is something you may well want two of, but one dry, sandy **desert** is enough."

# Try It!

Choose *desert, deserts,* or *dessert* for each ☐.
(See page 251 for answers.)

**1**. Please don't ☐ me on this dry, arid ☐.

**2.** They say that rats ☐ a sinking ship.

**3.** Harvey received his just ☐ tonight for his naughty behavior: no ☐ after supper and no TV or electronic games.

**4.** If you violate your orders and ☐ your military post, albeit in a sweltering, uninhabitable ☐, the army will see that you get your just ☐, which will be sweet, like a ☐ sweet.

**5.** He said he would never ☐ her, as they stood on their ☐ island, looking over the ocean for ships.

# DEVICE ... DEVISE

## Examples from Quotes

Democracy is a **device** that insures we shall be governed no better than we deserve.
— George Bernard Shaw

Building a mechanical **device** for its appearance is like putting lace on a bowling ball.
— Andrew Vachss

Human subtlety will never **devise** an invention more beautiful, more simple or more direct than does nature because in her inventions nothing is lacking, and nothing is superfluous.
— Leonardo da Vinci

My first care the following morning was to **devise** some means of discovering the man in the grey cloak. — Adelbert von Chamisso

## Dictionary Definitions

**device** *n.* A plan, gadget, or artistic contrivance devised to help accomplish one's purpose.

This *device* helps golfers improve their putting accuracy.

**devise** *v.* To form a plan; to invent, contrive.

We need to *devise* a method to increase revenue without increasing taxes.

## Memory Tricks

RHYME: This device is nice, but will it catch mice?

RHYME: Let's be **wise** and **devise** a **disguise.**

CONNECT the **c** in **devi̲ce** with the **c** in **c**ontraption.

CONNECT the **s** in **devi̲se** with the **s** in **s**cheme.

## Try It!

Choose *device* or *devise* for each ☐
(See page 251 for answers.)

**1.** He tried to ☐ a foolproof plan to pick the winning lottery number.

**2.** This state-of-the-art optical ☐ will enable you to read a newspaper from across a football field.

**3.** Can you ☐ a ☐ to open a padlock that has a combination lock?

**4.** During the Cold War, the proliferation of spies engendered a need to ☐ tools for spies.

**5.** The need to ☐ a ☐ to conceal a weapon produced the fake cigarette pack, a ☐ that concealed a one-shot 22 caliber pistol.

**6.** Since a spy may need to ☐ an escape plan, the CIA was able to successfully ☐ a unique means of escape, More than a simple ☐, it was an inflatable single-engine plane that inflated in under 6 minutes and could fly up to 70 mph.

69

# DISINTERESTED ... UNINTERESTED

 ## Examples from Quotes

I'm hardly **disinterested** totally in my appearance.
— *Frank Langella*

There is no such thing on earth as an uninteresting subject; the only thing that can exist is an **uninterested** person. — *Gilbert K. Chesterton*

You have reached the pinnacle of success as soon as you become **uninterested** in money, compliments, or publicity. — *Thomas Wolfe*

 ## Dictionary Definitions

**disinterested** *adj.* Impartial; neutral; having no stake in.

With a horse in the race, you're not a *disinterested* party.

**uninterested** *adj.* Not interested; bored; indifferent.

I love baseball but am totally *uninterested* in football.

 ## Memory Tricks

CONNECT: **disinterested** →**D**oesn't **I**nvolve **S**elf-**Interest**. (If you are not personally affected by something you can be impartial, **disinterested**.)

CONNECT: **uninterested** → **U**tterly **N**ot **I**nterested.

# Try It!

Choose *disinterested* or *uninterested* for each ☐.
(See page 252 for answers.)

**1.** We need impartial, ☐ fact-finders to help resolve this controversy.

**2.** I find it difficult to make myself study if I am ☐ in the subject.

**3.** Don't ask me about the mayoral race, since I am absolutely ☐ in politics.

**4.** Far from being ☐, Milbridge eats up local politics, although you might expect him to be a ☐ spectator, since he hails from the British Isles.

**5.** Since I am ☐ in anything to do with math, I am ☐ in taking a course in statistics.

**6.** To render a fair decision, a judge must be ☐ and impartial.

**7.** The ruler found it hard to get ☐ advice from any of his counselors.

**8.** He was ☐ in our discussion about local politics, but we tried to get his opinion as a ☐ citizen of another state.

## EFFECT *See* AFFECT

# E. G. ... I. E.

## Examples from Quotes

One and the same thing can at the same time be good, bad, and indifferent, **e.g.**, music is good to the melancholy, bad to those who mourn, and neither good nor bad to the deaf.— Baruch Spinoza

It has generally been assumed that of two opposing systems of philosophy, **e.g.**, realism and idealism, one only can be true and one must be false and so philosophers have been hopelessly divided on the question, which is the true one.
— Morris Raphael Cohen

The number of guests at dinner should not be less than the number of the Graces nor exceed that of the Muses, **i.e.**, it should begin with three and stop at nine.— Marcus Terentius Varro

The digestive canal represents a tube passing through the entire organism and communicating with the external world, **i.e.**, as it were the external surface of the body, but turned inwards and thus hidden in the organism. — Ivan Pavlov

## Dictionary Definitions

**e.g.** *abbr.* (Latin: *exempli gratia*) For example.

This diet includes foods rich in fiber, *e.g.*, bran, oatmeal, and raw vegetables.

**i.e.** *abbr.* (Latin: *id est*) That is.

That diet limits daily intake of carbohydrates, *i.e.,* starches and sugars.

# Memory Tricks

MISPRONOUNCE: Say "**eg**g zample" to remember that *e.g.* stands for "for example."

CONNECT the *i* in *i.e.* to the *i* in "that *is*."

# Try It!

Choose *e.g.* or *i.e.* for each ☐.
(See page 252 for answers.)

**1.** The fourth president of the United States, ☐, James Madison, served for two terms.

**2.** Some insects can sting, ☐, ants, bees, wasps, and hornets.

**3.** Tourist attractions, ☐, beaches, resort casinos, Revolutionary War sites, and the Pine Barrens, abound in the Garden State, ☐, New Jersey.

**4.** Ascorbic acid, ☐, Vitamin C, helps heal wounds and aids in maintaining health, ☐, by resisting infection from certain viruses and bacteria.

**5.** There is a vaccine available for pertussis, ☐, whooping cough, which is a highly contagious disease spread through the air, ☐, by coughing, sneezing, or breathing in someone's face.

# ELICIT ... ILLICIT

## Examples from Quotes

The test of leadership is not to put greatness into humanity, but to **elicit** it, for the greatness is already there. — *James Buchanan*

You can **elicit** much more sympathy from friends over a bad marriage than you ever can from a good divorce. — *P. J. O'Rourke*

Never seek **illicit** wealth. — *Confucius*

I think everyone recognizes that **illicit** financial activities are threats to all of our financial systems. — *Daniel Glaser*

## Dictionary Definitions

**elicit** *v.* To draw forth; bring out.

Angie's sad story was designed to *elicit* sympathy.

**illicit** *adj.* Illegal; not permitted.

The bill cracks down on *illicit* drug use.

## Memory Tricks

CONNECT: **elicit** → **e**voke → **e**vacuate → **e**vict.

Connect: **illicit** → **ill**egal → **ill**egitimate

# Try It!

Choose *elicit* or *illicit* for each ☐.
(See page 253 for answers.)

**1.** ☐ copies of the CD will ☐ outrage if we sell it.

**2.** His quote is sure to ☐ outrage if we print it.

**3.** We must ☐ public support to stop ☐ sales of cigarettes to minors.

**4.** When his ☐ investment scheme is exposed, it is sure to ☐ angry responses from irate investors.

**5.** Once the senator's ☐ tax-evasion scheme is exposed, it is doubtful that she will still ☐ the support of her constituents.

**6.** The sales letter did not ☐ any responses yet.

**7.** The arrest was for possession of ☐ drugs.

**8.** The phone calls were intended to ☐ information on how people were going to vote.

**9.** This photo of the sad-eyed puppy is guaranteed to ☐ sympathy.

**10.** The police confiscated over $200,000 in ☐ profits made in his ☐ business activities.

**11.** What information does the survey intend to ☐ from the respondents?

# EMIGRATE ... IMMIGRATE

## Examples from Quotes

If ever again I see this land, I hope it will be with a Fenian band; So God be with old Ireland! Poor Pat must **emigrate**.— "Poor Pat Must Emigrate," 19th Century Irish Ballad

The hunger for land was another motivating factor for the Palatine **emigration**. . . . The realization that they would have to **emigrate** to accomplish that goal made them willing to listen to British propaganda about the New World.
— *Kathryn Parker*

Contrary to what people might expect, the desire to **immigrate** is not restricted to the poor.
— *Roberto Suro*

I think we should modify the laws to a point where it doesn't take several years to **immigrate**.
— *Jack Jackson*

## Dictionary Definitions

**emigrate** *v.* To leave one's own counry or region to settle in another.

Giovanni has decided to *emigrate* from his native Italy to the United States.

**immigrate** *v.* To enter a country of which one is not a native to establish residency.

He is going to *immigrate* to the United States from Italy.

# Memory Tricks

CONNECT the **e** in **emigrate** with the **e** in **exit**. When you **emigrate**, you "**exit**" your country.

CONNECT: **immigrate** → **im**port, "to bring into a country."

CONNECT: Both **immigrate** and **in** begin with **i**.

# Try It!

Choose *emigrate* or *immigrate* for each ❑.
(See page 253 for answers.)

**1.** If you ❑ from the United States and ❑ to Canada, will you lose your U.S. citizenship?

**2.** In 1849, the California Gold Rush prompted poverty-stricken laborers to ❑ from China and ❑ to the United States.

**3.** By the 1870s, gold had become scarce, the economy was in a steep decline, and laborers who been lured to ❑ to California became scapegoats.

**4.** In particular, animosity was directed toward those who had been lured to ❑ from China.

**5.** This resulted in the Chinese Exclusion Act, which barred those who tried to ❑ from China and ❑ to the United States.

**6.** In 1795 they decided to ❑ from their homeland and ❑ to America.

# EMPATHY ... SYMPATHY

 ## Examples from Quotes

I have absolutely no **empathy** for camels. I didn't care for being abused in the Middle East by those horrible, horrible, horrible creatures.
— *Rachel Weisz*

I look for a role that hopefully I feel **empathy** with and that I can understand and love, but also that has challenge for me to play — a different kind of role, a different type of character, a different time period. — *Kathy Bates*

And whoever walks a furlong without **sympathy** walks to his own funeral drest in his shroud.
— *Walt Whitman*

Autumn wins you best by this, its mute appeal to **sympathy** for its decay. — *Robert Browning*

 ## Dictionary Definitions

**empathy** *n.* An understanding of the feelings, thoughts, and motives of another.

I feel *empathy* for Lee, but I don't feel as she does.

**sympathy** *n.* The act of or capacity for sharing another's feelings.

I am torn by compassion and *sympathy* for the suffering of that unfortunate child.

## Memory Tricks

CONNECT THE **s** in **s**ympathy with **s**orrow for **s**omeone or **s**omething (without experiencing that person's feelings).

 ## Try It!

Choose *empathy* or *sympathy* for each ❑.
(See page 254 for answers.)

**1.** They were deeply moved by ❑ for the sufferings of the flood victims.

**2.** It is hard to feel ❑ for someone whose misfortune was caused by his own reckless behavior.

**3.** I feel ❑ for those who have a fear of public speaking even though I don't suffer from that particular phobia.

**4.** The teacher has ❑ for students who have reading comprehension difficulties.

**5.** He struggled to find words to express his heartfelt ❑.

**6.** He expressed ❑ for the earthquake victims.

**7.** Please accept our ❑ for your loss.

## ENSURE *See* ASSURE

# EVERY DAY ... EVERYDAY

 ## Examples from Quotes

It is easier to be a lover than a husband for the simple reason that it is more difficult to be witty **every day** than to say pretty things from time to time. — *Honore de Balzac*

I have no dress except the one I wear. If you are going to be kind enough to give me one, please let it be practical and dark so that I can put it on afterwards to go to the laboratory **every day**. — *Marie Curie*

Hippocrates is an excellent geometer but a complete fool in **everyday** affairs. — *Aristotle*

 ## Dictionary Definitions

**every day** *adj. + n,* Daily; happening each day.

My cat insists that I feed her *every day* at 7:00 A.M.

**everyday** *adj.* Usual; ordinary.

The novel was just another *everyday* psychological thriller.

 ## Memory Tricks

SUBSTITUTE: Try substituting ***every* <u>single</u> *day*** for the word in question. If that works, use the two-word version, **every day**.

SUBSTITUTE: Try substituting <u>ordinary</u> for the word in question. If it works, use the one-word version, **everyday.**

# Try It!

Choose *every day* or *everyday* for each for each ☐.
(See page 254 for answers.)

**1.** George follows the same routine ☐ when he wakes up.

**2.** Since the dance is not formal, you may wear your ☐ clothes.

**3.** If you use this product faithfully ☐, you will be amazed at the results.

**4.** Undoubtedly you have discovered that ☐ remedies don't work.

**5.** You can apply lemon juice to your freckles ☐, and the only benefit will be to the lemon growers.

**6.** We receive glowing reports from users of Freckles Be Gone ☐.

**7.** Since the sun shines ☐, slap on some Freckles Be Gone as an ☐ precaution before venturing outside.

**8.** Make Freckles Be Gone part of your ☐ skin care program, and your skin will thank you ☐.

# EVERY ONE ... EVERYONE

 ## Examples from Quotes

I have written **every one** of my novels to convince somebody of something. — *Manuel Puig*

I believe **every one** of us possesses a fundamental right to tell our own story. — *Joyce Maynard*

All right, **everyone**, line up alphabetically according to your height. — *Casey Stengel*

 ## Dictionary Definitions

**every one** *adj. + pron.* Each person or thing in a group.

Alvin ate *every one* of the green jelly beans.

**everyone** *pron.* Everybody.

Has *everyone* signed the attendance sheet?

USAGE NOTE: *Every one* is used when the sense refers to each individual member of a specific group. *Everyone* is used in the sense of "everybody without exception." Each word takes a singular pronoun and a singular verb.

 ## Memory Trick

SUBSTITUTE: If you can substitute *everybody* for the word in question, use the one-word version: ***everyone.*** If not, use ***every one.***

# Try It!

Choose *every one* or *everyone* for each ☐.
(See page 255 for answers.)

**1.** A fad is something that sweeps ☐ away for a brief time before it fades away and ☐ of its devotees forgets about it.

**2.** In 1958, when Wham-O, Inc. introduced its Hula Hoop® to America, ☐ of the first twenty million was sold in six months for $1.98 each.

**3.** During the 1960s, with the Hula Hoop® craze in full swing, ☐ who had hips and the inclination was hula hooping.

**4.** Not ☐ who tried to hula hoop succeeded.

**5.** The hip rotating craze was not admired by ☐, as evidenced by Japan's banning it on the grounds of indecency.

**6.** On March 3, 1939, Harvard freshman Lothrop Withington, Jr., swallowed a live goldfish on a $10 bet, starting a craze that ☐ condemned.

**7.** Goldfish swallowing soon swamped college campuses and was indulged in by ☐ game enough to try it.

**8.** Image the outrage of ☐ who had ever owned or admired a goldfish!

**EXCEPT** *See* **ACCEPT**

**EXCUSE** *See* **ALIBI**

# FARTHER ... FURTHER

 ## Examples from Quotes

The **farther** backward you can look the **farther** forward you can see. — *Winston Churchill*

If I have seen **farther** than others, it is because I was standing on the shoulders of giants.
— *Isaac Newton*

A mediocre idea that generates enthusiasm will go **further** than a great idea that inspires no one.
— *Mary Kay Ash*

Gratitude is merely the secret hope of **further** favors. — *Françoise de la Rochefoucauld*

 ## Dictionary Definitions

**farther** *adv.* To or at a more distant point in time or space.

Let's drive fifty miles *farther* before we stop to eat.

**further** *adv.* 1. More; to a greater extent. 2. In addition to; furthermore.

We need to explore this matter *further* before we decide.

USAGE NOTE: In informal usage, *further* may substitute for *farther* to refer to physical distance. The reverse is not true, however. for *farther*. It is incorrect to say, "We'll discuss this *farther*."

## Memory Tricks

CONNECT: *farther* → **far,** "near and **far**", and "**far** away" to remember that *farther* refers to physical distance.

CONNECT: *further* →*further*more. Think: "*Further* means "more"; it also means "*further*more."

## Try It!

Choose *farther* or *further* for each ◻.
(See page 255 for answers.)

**1.** In the 1920s, astronaut Edwin Hubbell discovered that galaxies around us were moving ◻ from the Earth.

**2.** ◻, by observing patterns of color in the sky and how those colors shifted in the nearer and ◻ galaxies, he was led to the conclusion that the universe was expanding uniformly. In 1998, using larger telescopes, astronomers made a ◻ discovery. The ◻ galaxies were moving ◻ away from Earth much faster than expected. Yes, the universe was expanding, but ◻, the expansion was accelerating.

**3.** The ◻ ahead we look in time, the ◻ the distance between galaxies.

**4.** If we could look ◻ into the future, we might see it happening in approximately a trillion times a fifty-year lifespan.

85

# FEWER ... LESS

## Examples from Quotes

The **fewer** the words, the better the prayer.
— *Martin Luther*

I always say that bad women are **fewer** than bad men, but when you get one, they're fascinating because they're so rotten. — *Ann Rule*

Resolve not to be poor; whatever you have, spend **less**. — *Samuel Johnson*

Humility is not thinking **less** of yourself, it's thinking of yourself **less**. — *Rick Warren*

## Dictionary Definitions

**fewer** *adj.* A smaller number of persons or things.

Eating *fewer* calories generally results in weight loess

**less** *adj.* A more limited amount in magnitude or degree.

There is *less* water in the lake this year.

NOTE: Traditionally, *fewer* is used for things that can be counted and *less* for collective nouns and abstract concepts. Amounts of time, distance, and money use *less* when they are thought of as a single unit (collectively): *less* than three months; *less* than 9 feet; *less* than $150,000.

# Memory Tricks

VISUALIZE & RHYME: (Visualize yourself comparing your two new sports cars with a garage-full of old "clunkers.") My cars may be *fewer*, but they are *newer*.

RHYME: To remind yourself that *less* refers to things that can't be counted, think, "*Less mess* means *less stress.*"

## Try It!

Choose *fewer* or *less* for each ❑.
(See page 256 for answers.)

**1.** In 1793 the French adopted a metric 10-hour day, so that a day had 14 hours ❑ than before.

**2.** Although each day had ❑ hours, each hour had no ❑ time because an hour was 100 minutes. In addition every month had three weeks, which was ❑ weeks than before.

**3.** Each week had 10 days, so that every month had 30 days. No month had ❑.

**4.** A logical system, *n'est-ce pas?* Seemingly, it would cause ❑ confusion and ❑ missed appointments.

**5.** The system, a triumph of French logic, was not to last but was abandoned by no ❑ a personage than Napoleon Bonaparte, shortly after he was crowned emperor in 1804.

# FOREWORD ... FORWARD

 **Examples from Quotes**

I was thinking of writing a little **foreword** saying that history is, after all, based on people's recollections, which change with time.
— *Frederik Pohl*

Here I am, a nice Jewish mother, writing the **foreword** for a book about Christian nice guys.
— *Laura Schlessinger*

Don't hold back. Don't be shy. Step **forward** in every way you can to plan boldly, to speak clearly, to offer the leadership which the world needs.
— *Claudia Lady Byrd Johnson*

We do not move **forward** by curtailing people's liberty because we are afraid of what they may do or say. — *Eleanor Roosevelt*

**foreword** n, An introductory statement at the beginning of a book, usually written by someone other than the author.

The book's *foreword* was written by a noted Egyptologist.

**forward** adj. 1. At or near the front. 2. Moving toward the front. 3. Ardent, impudent. v. To assist or send onward.

The line moved *forward* at a snail's pace.

That young man is unpleasantly brash and *forward.*

I will *forward* your remarks to Senator Hodges.

# Memory Tricks

CONNECT the **"word"** in *foreword* to a book.

CONNECT: *forward* → *back**ward***. This pair of antonyms end in *–ward,* which indicates a direction. They are not related in meaning to the word *"word."*

# Try It!

Choose *foreword* or *forward* for each ☐.
(See page 256 for answers.)

**1.** The preface of a book is written by the author, but the book's ☐ is written by someone else.

**2.** We cannot move ☐ until we agree on a plan.

**3.** After reading the book's intriguing ☐, I looked ☐ to reading what the author had to say.

**4.** I wanted to find out for myself whether the book's ☐ had exaggerated the book's appeal to ☐-thinking readers, who envision moving ☐ to the day when humans colonize Mars.

**5.** Always put your best foot ☐.

**6.** I will be honored to write the ☐.

**7.** He leaned ☐ to hear what she was saying.

**8.** A famous American historian wrote the ☐ to the second edition.

# FORMALLY ... FORMERLY

## Examples from Quotes

I was an accidental actor. I was never **formally** trained. — *David Soul*

I **formally** proposed. I'm a good Southern gentleman. — *Vince Gill*

By recollecting the pleasures I have had **formerly**, I renew them, I enjoy them a second time, while I - laugh at the remembrance of troubles now past, and which I no longer feel. — *Giacomo Casanova*

I was **formerly** so stuck into plans. I can now live more spontaneously. — *Gabriela Sabatini*

## Dictionary Definitions

**formally** *adv.* Following accepted forms or conventions.

We haven't been *formally* introduced.

Although not *formally* trained, she became a famed singer.

**formerly** *adv.* At a former time.

Wasn't he *formerly* known as Prince?

# Memory Tricks

CONNECT **formally** → **formal**. Think, "Dress *formally* for the *formal* dinner.

RHYME: Although you're dressed *formally*, please try to act **normally**.

CONNECT *formerly* → *former*.

TONGUE TWISTER: Although Frank's flabby now, he was *formerly* firmer.

 # Try It!

Choose *formally* or *formerly* for each ☐.
(See page 257 for answers.)

**1.** He was ☐ known as "Sweeney" before ☐ changing his name.

**2.** Although I never replied ☐ to his written invitation, I ☐ mentioned to him that I would attend his graduation.

**3.** Winthorpe, ☐ casual and careless about his appearance, was transformed after meeting the ☐ elegant Caroline.

**4.** His ☐ disreputable trench coat was gone, and in its place, a ☐ cut Savile Row topcoat, the apotheosis of elegance and style.

# FORTUITOUS ... FORTUNATE

 ## Examples from Quotes

*Fortuitous* circumstances constitute the molds that shape the majority of human lives, and the happy impress of an accident is too often regarded as the relentless decree of all ordaining fate.
— *Olympia Brown*

It's good to keep in mind that prominence is always a mix of hard work, eloquence in your practice, good timing and *fortuitous* social relations.
— *Barbara Kruger*

Do not speak of your happiness to one less *fortunate* than yourself. — *Plutarch*

Alas for the affairs of men! When they are *fortunate* you might compare them to a shadow; and if they are unfortunate, a wet sponge with one dash wipes the picture away. — *Aeschylus*

 ## Dictionary Definitions

**fortuitous** *adj.* Happening completely by accident or chance.

How *fortuitous* to miss my flight and chance to meet you!

She was born under a *fortuitous* conjunction of the stars.

**fortunate** *adj.* Bringing or receiving unforeseen good fortune; lucky.

Indeed, I feel *fortunate* to be the recipient of this award.

We were *fortunate* to find such good Italian bread.

USAGE NOTE: Something *fortuitous* happens entirely by chance. It can also be *fortunate*, but it is imprecise to use *fortuitous* without indicating the operation of chance.

## Memory Tricks

RHYME: A stroke of luck, how ***fortuitous!*** I may become quite *platit**udinous**.*

ALLITERATION: ***Fortunate F**red **f**ound his **f**uture in a **fortune** cookie.*

## Try It!

Choose *fortuitous* or *fortunate* for each ☐.
(See page 257 for answers.)

**1.** The ☐ circumstance of having a doctor in the house was truly ☐.

**2.** How ☐ to find that money just when I needed it!

**3.** She is indeed ☐ to have a supportive family.

**4.** Taking that advanced biology course turned out to be ☐.

**5.** This new bill is designed to help the less ☐.

**6.** It was ☐ we left before the blizzard arrived.

**FORWARD** *See* **FOREWORD**

**FURTHER** *See* **FARTHER**

# GOOD ... WELL

## Examples from Quotes

Fewer things are harder to put up with in life than a **good** example. — *Mark Twain*

If you look **good** and dress *well,* you don't need a purpose in life. — *Robert Pante*

Doing a thing **well** is often a waste of time.
— *Robert Byrne*

The game of life is not so much in holding a **good** hand as playing a poor hand **well**. — *H. T. Leslie*

 **Dictionary Definitions**

**good** *adj.* Having favorable or suitable qualities.

If we have *good* weather it will be a *good* day at the beach.

Today looks like a *good* day to go fishing.

**well** *adv.* 1. Satisfactorily; skillfully.
2. Comfortably; advantageously. 3. Properly; prudently.

Ted is a *good* musician who plays the trombone and trumpet extremely *well.*

She wanted to hire someone whose qualifications were *well* suited for the position being advertised.

You would do *well* to mind your manners.

## Memory Tricks

ACRONYM: Here is a **good** TIP: **T**hings, **I**deas, and
  **P**eople can be **good.**
MISPRONOUNCE: *"**Vell** goes vit a verb."* (**Well** goes
  with a verb.)

 ## Try It!

Choose *good* or *well* for each ❏.
(See page 257 for the answers.)

Typically, during severe droughts lightning
ignites wildfires that ravage the Okefenokee
Swamp. Since ❏ methods of fire retardation work
❏ to combat wildfires, it would be a ❏ idea to use
them. Right? Not necessarily. Natural fires are ❏
for the Okefenokee and are necessary to keep the
swamp "healthy" and ❏. In fact, without wildfires,
the Okefenokee would cease to exist. Fires clear
the swamp of shrubs, small trees, and layers of
peat several feet deep, whose gradual buildup
would otherwise choke the swamp. The burning of
peat has a ❏ result. It reveals open lakes. The
destruction of small trees is ❏ for the growth of the
classic tree of the Okefenokee, the large cypress
(which is fire resistant.) As far as wildfires in the
Okefenokee are concerned, perhaps it's fair to say
that all's ❏ that ends ❏.

# HANGED ... HUNG

 **Examples from Quotes**

> He who wishes to be rich in a day will be **hanged** in a year. — *Leonardo da Vinci*
>
> No man has ever yet been **hanged** for breaking the spirit of a law. — *Grover Cleveland*
>
> A room **hung** with pictures is a room **hung** with thoughts. — *Joshua Reynolds*
>
> Now like the old Irish minstrel, I have **hung** up my harp because my songs are all sung.
> — *John McCormack*

**hanged** or **hung** *v.* Both are past-tense forms of the verb *hang,* meaning "to suspend from above with no support below."

USAGE NOTE: *Hanged* is the preferred form when the object of the hanging is a person. People are *hanged*; objects are *hung.*

> The king ordered the traitors to be *hanged.*
>
> The stockings were *hung* by the chimney.

 **Memory Tricks**

VISUALIZE: Picture the hangman's noose that is drawn for the word game "Hangman" to remember that **hanged** refers to death of a person by hanging.

CONNECT **hung** with "The stockings were **hung** by the chimney with care," to associate **hung** with objects.

## Try It!

Choose *hanged* or *hung* for each ☐.
(See page 258 for answers.)

**1.** We washed the muddy clothes and ☐ them out to dry.

**2.** The outlaw was sentenced to be ☐.

**3.** When hanging pictures, use a level to make sure they are ☐ straight.

**4.** The famous "hanging judge," Arkansas's Isaac Parker, ordered 160 executions, of which 79 were carried out and the 79 sentenced were ☐.

**5.** The keys were ☐ on hooks attached to the closet door.

**6.** During the days of the "Old West," many of the outlaws were ☐.

**7.** The man convinced of poisoning the king was ☐.

**8.** I almost ☐ up the phone, but the urgency in her voice made me decide to hang on.

**9.** They were ☐ when their assassination plot was discovered.

# HEALTHFUL ... HEALTHY

 ## Examples from Quotes

> Drinking freshly made juices and eating enough whole foods to provide adequate fiber is a sensible approach to a **healthful** diet. — *Jay Kordich*

> Sugar in moderation has a place in a **healthful** lifestyle. — *Charles Baker*

> The dignity of the physician requires that he should look **healthy**. — *Hippocrates*

> A **healthy** male adult bore consumes each year one and a half times his own weight in other people's patience. — *John Updike*

 ## Dictionary Definitions

**healthful** *adj.* Beneficial to health; conducive to good health.

> In general, is it more *healthful* to eat vegetables raw rather than fried?

**healthy** *adj.* Possessing good health. 2. Conducive to good health.

> The puppies were lively and appeared to be *healthy*.

> Before this, he had always been *healthy*.

USAGE NOTE: In common usage, *healthy* is used is used as a synonym for *healthful* when referring to things or activities that benefit health, e.g., "*healthy* air." Strictly speaking, however, *healthful* should be used to mean "promoting health."

 ## Memory Tricks

CONNECT: Think, "I want to be **healthy**, wealthy, and wise.

CONTRAST: Living things can be **healthy**. Nonliving things and activities can be **healthful**.

 ## Try It!

Choose *healthful* or *healthy* for each ☐.
(See page 258 for answers.)

**1**. Which is more ☐, cheesecake or fried green tomatoes?

**2**. If you want to be ☐, exercise regularly.

**3**. Eat a ☐ diet in order to achieve optimum health and stay ☐.

**4**. Here the ☐ climate attracts those who want to feel ☐ again.

**5**. These ☐ foods should be included in your diet on your road to health.

**6**. You need to cut down on sugar and eat ☐ foods if you want to be ☐.

**7**. Eat a ☐ diet, exercise regularly, and get a good night's sleep to stay ☐.

# HISTORIC ... HISTORICAL

 **Examples from Quotes**

Now, 0 for 50 would be a **historic** achievement on any other team, but on the Cubs it is usually called September. — *Bernie Lincicome*

If I can generate enough income, I'd like to get a castle, a **historic** castle that I can restore. — *Henry Thomas*

Fable is more **historical** than fact, because fact tells us about one man and fable tells us about a million men. — *Gilbert K. Chesterton*

 **Dictionary Definitions**

**historic** *adj.* Having importance or fame in history; famous.

> The signing of the war treaty was a *historic* event.

> A monument was erected at the *historic* battle site.

**historical** *adj.* Of or related to history; having the characteristics of history; based on history.

> This *historical* novel takes place in the antebellum South.

> The date of Thomas Jefferson's birth is a *historical* fact.

USAGE NOTE: *Historic* refers to something important to history, e.g., a *historic* event. Something related to history is *historical*, e.g., a *historical* novel.

# Memory Tricks

CONNECT: **historic** → **historic** moment, **historic** event.

CONNECT: **historical** → **historical** novel, **historical** character. Think: "I would like to write a *hysterical* **historical** novel."

# Try It!

Choose *historic* o59 for answers.)

1. The letter is not a ☐ document. Its ☐ interest lies in the fact that it was written by Martha Washington.

2. The famous phrase "the shot heard 'round the world" is a ☐ reference to the opening shot of the Revolutionary War.

3. That ☐ shot was fired on April 19, 1775, in Lexington, Massachusetts when the British encountered American militiamen who refused to disperse.

4. Although there is no ☐ evidence as to who fired that ☐ shot, it was followed by others, and eight Americans lay dead.

5. That ☐ event in Lexington marked the beginning of America's fight for independence.


**HUNG** *See* **HANGED**

# I ... ME

 ## Examples from Quotes

My partner and **I** won the race, and **I** threw my hat into the air and bent to pick it up. — *Chris LeDoux*

Will **I** wait a lonely lifetime? If you want **me** to, **I** will. — *The Beatles*

There is only one difference between a madman and **me**. **I** am not mad. — *Salvador Dali*

Tell **me** and **I** forget. Teach **me** and **I** remember. Involve **me** and **I** learn. — *Benjamin Franklin*

Sometimes **I** lie awake at night and ask, "Where have **I** gone wrong?" Then a voice says to **me**----- "This is going to take more than one night. — *Charles M. Schulz*

 ## Dictionary Definitions

**I** *pro.* The subject pronoun used to represent the speaker or writer.

Sydney and *I* volunteered to help with the food drive.

**me** *pro.* The object pronoun used to represent the speaker or writer (i.e., the object of a verb or a prepositional phrase).

Herb invited Michelle, Chad, and *me* to the party.

USAGE NOTE: A common error is to use *I* instead of *me* after a preposition.

> Correct: "between him and *me*" (*me* = object of "between").

> Incorrect: "between him and *I.*"

 ## Memory Tricks

SIMPLIFY: Mentally remove any other pronouns or nouns: "(Jenny and) **I** volunteered to help," "Herb invited (Jeff and) **me.**" This helps to decide whether to use **I** or **me**.

PLACEMENT: **I** comes before an action verb; **me** comes after an action verb or preposition: "**I** see you. Do you see **me**?"

 ## Try It!

Choose *I* or *me* for each ☐.
(See page 260 for answers.)

**1.** Maurice and ☐ went back to Boston, where he and ☐ first met.

**2.** Do you believe him or ☐?

**3.** Between you and ☐, George, Andrea, and ☐ are enlisting in the navy.

**4.** Will you feed the dog for Bernie and ☐ if he and ☐ decide to go to the fair?

**5.** Among Dean, Josh, Greg, and ☐, only Dean and ☐ ordered dessert.

# IMPLY ... INFER

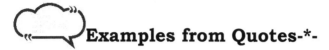**Examples from Quotes-*-**

But the fact that some geniuses were laughed at does not **imply** that all who are laughed at are geniuses. — *Carl Sagan*

Contrary to what many writers **imply** about the process, nobody forces a writer to sell his work to the film industry. — *Thomas Perry*

From a drop of water, a logician could **infer** the possibility of an Atlantic or a Niagara without having seen or heard of one or the other.
— *Arthur Conan Doyle*

We observe closely related species in sympathy and **infer** how they evolved from a common ancestor.
— *Peter R. Grant*

 **Dictionary Definitions**

**imply** *v.* To suggest; to express indirectly.

Did the article *imply* that the senator is becoming senile?

I did not mean to *imply* that you are always late.

**infer** *v.* To draw a conclusion or inference.

A broken window led police to *infer* it was a forced entry.

# Memory Tricks

Speakers and writer **imply**. They can hint, suggest. Readers and listeners **infer**. They can deduce, come to a conclusion.

THINK: **I** (as a speaker or writer) **imply**.
**You** (as a reader or listener) **infer**.

# Try It!

Choose *imply* or *infer* for each ☐.
(See page 260 for answers.)

**1.** What clues lead you to ☐ that Schultz has recently visited India?

**2.** Does that raised eyebrow ☐ you are a skeptic in regard to astrology?

**3.** I hope you did not ☐ from my remark that I think you should diet. "Pleasingly plump" was not meant to ☐ anything of the kind.

**4.** Indeed, we may ☐ from numerous examples in the animal kingdom that the tendency to store fat may ☐ a superior genetic ability to survive famine.

**5.** You may ☐, however, that I meant to ☐ that I find you pleasingly attractive.

**6.** I hope you will ☐ that my awkwardly stated remark was meant as a compliment.

105

# ITS ... IT'S

## Examples from Quotes

This country, with **its** institutions, belongs to the people who inhabit it. — *Abraham Lincoln*

Government, even in **its** best state, is but a necessary evil; in **its** worst state, an intolerable one. — *Thomas Paine*

**It's** like déjà-vu, all over again. — *Yogi Berra*

**It's** not that I'm so smart, **it's** just that I stay with problems longer. — *Albert Einstein*

## Dictionary Definitions

**its** *adj.* Possessive form of the pronoun *it.*

The beagle opened *its* mouth to let out a mournful howl.

Can you tell a book by *its* cover?

**it's** Contraction of *it is* or *it has.*

Who says *it's* always sunny in Philadelphia?

If *it's* not broken, why fix it?

*It's* been said that you can't teach an old dog new tricks.

USAGE NOTE: A common mistake is to use *it's* to show possession. This is a logical error because a noun adds *apostrophe-s* to show possession. This method does not work with *it,* however, because *it* is a pronoun. Pronouns have special forms to show possession. The possessive form of *it* is *its.*

## Memory Tricks

LOGICAL EXTENSION: You wouldn't write *m'y, hi's,* or *he'r* to show possession. The same is true for **its**.

GRAMMAR: Contractions reflect speech. The apostrophe stands for the letter or letters that are omitted when words are run together in speech. We say **it's** instead of *it is* or *it has.* Thus, write **it's** only if you mean *it is* or *it has.*

## Try It!

Choose *its* or *it's* for each ☐.
(See page 260 for the answers).

**1.** If ☐ Tuesday, this must be Belgium.

**2.** Can you name this place? ☐ name comes from the Middle English word for "rabbit."

**3.** ☐ been called "America's Playground," known worldwide for ☐ hot dogs, ☐ Cyclone Roller Coaster, Mermaid Parade, and Deno's Wonderwheel. ☐ the one and only Coney Island. ☐ reputation was well deserved.

**IMMIGRATE** *See* **EMIGRATE**
**INSURE** *See* **ASSURE**
**IRRITATE** *See* **AGGRAVATE**

# JEALOUS ... ZEALOUS

 ## Examples from Quotes

It is matrimonial suicide to be **jealous** when you have a really good reason. — *Clare Boothe Luce*

Being in the room with an insanely **jealous** person is like being in the room with a dead mammoth. — *Mike Nichols*

A **zealous** sense of mission is only possible where there is opposition to it. — *D. W. Ewing*

People are **zealous** for a cause when they are not quite positive that it is true. — *Bertrand Russell*

 ## Dictionary Definitions

**jealous** *adj.* 1. Fearful of loss of affection or position. 2. Envious. 3. Vigilant in guarding a possession.

St. Augustine said that he that is *jealous* is not in love.

Those gossips are just *jealous* of your success.

**zealous** *adj.* Filled with eagerness; fervent.

The dog kept a *zealous* watch over its bone.

The young lawyer is a *zealous* advocate for her client.

# Memory Tricks

ALLITERATION: "Are you **jealous** of my _jewels,_
_Jaguar,_ and _jet?_

CONNECT: **zealous** → **zeal** → **zeal**ot.

# Try It!

Choose _jealous_ or _zealous_ for each ☐.
(See page 261 for answers.)

**1.** A ☐ reporter exposed corrupt officials who had taken kickbacks.

**2.** Wishing to appear ☐, Frank made a show of taking work home every night.

**3.** Would you be ☐ if I told you I had just won the Power Ball lottery?

**4.** Catherine was a fervent and ☐ reformer and was known to be a ☐ advocate of women's rights.

**5.** In spite of Alvin's ☐ attempts to get to the root of her problem, Alvina continued to feel ☐ and insecure in their relationship.

**6.** Geraldine had become increasingly ☐ in her determined attempts to reform Fred.

**7.** He was a ☐ defender of his beliefs, in spite of almost overwhelming resistance.

# JUDICIAL ... JUDICIOUS

 **Examples from Quotes**

No matter how badly senators want to know things, **judicial** nominees are limited in what they may discuss. — *Orrin Hatch*

The people in general ought to have regard to the moral character of those whom they invest with authority either in the legislative, executive, or **judicial** branches. — *John Witherspoon*

Advertising—a **judicious** mixture of flattery and threats. — *Northrop Frye*

A good father believes that he does wisely to encourage enterprise, productive skill, prudent self-denial, and **judicious** expenditure on the part of his son. — *William Graham Sumner*

 **Dictionary Definitions**

**judicial** *adj.* Of or pertaining to courts of law or the administration of justice.

The *judicial* branch is one of the three branches of federal government.*

**judicious** *adj.* Having or exhibiting sound judgment.

His *judicious* use of humor lightened his severe criticism.

# Memory Tricks

CONNECT: **judicial** → **judge** → **judg**ment.

RHYME: Think, "Be ambitious and **judicious**, not malicious or seditious."

## Try It!

Choose *judicial* or *judicious* for each ❑.
(See page 261 for answers.)

**1.** Do you believe that all juries are ❑ in rendering a verdict or in awarding damage awards?

**2.** Was it ❑ for an Austin, Texas, jury to award $780,000 to a woman who broke her ankle tripping over her toddler in a furniture store?

**3.** If lawyers would be more ❑ in the cases they accept, our ❑ system would not be swamped with frivolous lawsuits.

**4.** Lawyers were ❑ in refusing to accept the $380 million lawsuit against Michael Jordan by a man who claimed Jordan looked like him.

**5.** A ❑ use of mouthwash is recommended for garlic lovers in Indiana, where it is illegal to enter a movie theater or public streetcar within four hours of eating garlic.

**6.** Perhaps the Vermont law requiring citizens to take at least one bath a week—on Saturday night—should be subjected to ❑ review.

# KEY ... QUAY

## Examples from Quotes

People say that money is not the **key** to happiness, but I always figured if you have enough money, you can have a **key** made. — *Joan Rivers*

Everybody that visits the (Florida) **Keys** wants **key** lime pie. — *Charlene Griffin*

And mornin's going to me work, I meets her (my wife) on the **quay.** — *L. A. G. Strong*

## Dictionary Definitions

**key** *n.* 1. An instrument that opens a lock. 2. Something that provides new information, an explanation, or a solution. 3. An offshore island or a reef.

The padlock doesn't have a *key,* and I don't have the combination to open it.

The *key* to the code was simple—once we figured it out.

Let's take the boat and head out to the *key* for a picnic.

**quay** *n.* A wharf or landing place built parallel to a waterway to unload ships.

The ship pulled up to the *quay* to be unloaded.

# Memory Tricks

CONNECT: **key** → **key**hole → **key**note → **key**stone.

CONNECT the **a** in **quay** to the **a**'s in *wh<u>a</u>rf*. in *w<u>a</u>ter*, and in *b<u>a</u>nk*.

# Try It!

Choose *key(s)* or *quay(s)* for each ☐.
(See page 262 for answers.)

**1.** We walked along the wide cement ☐ that paralleled the riverbank.

**2.** The ☐ to relaxation is deep breathing.

**3.** I think this skeleton ☐ will unlock the door at the back of the shed.

**4.** This small red feather is the ☐ to the solution of the mystery.

**5.** As she was getting off the ship docked at the ☐, the ☐ to her car fell from her hand and into the murky water.

**6.** Those small islands are the ☐ I was referring to, not the ☐ to the cabin.

**7.** You will find beautiful ornamental gardens and sandy beaches on the ☐.

# LAY ... LIE

## Examples from Quotes

Admittedly, I traveled with a sleeping bag, but I could always find somewhere to **lay** my head.
— *Jeremy Irons*

I **lay** on my bed at the hospital and said. "Let's see what I have left." And I could see, I could speak, I could think, I could read. — *Dale Evans*

I should like to **lie** at your feet and die in your arms. — *Voltaire*

It is better to take what does not belong to you than let it **lie** around neglected. — *Mark Twain*

The secret of staying young is to live honestly, eat slowly, and **lie** about your age. — *Lucille Ball*

## Dictionary Definitions

**lay** *v.* 1. To place or put. 2. Past tense of "to *lie*" ("to recline"). 3. To produce and deposit ("*lay* eggs").

Please *lay* the dirty dishes on the counter.

Last night I *lay* down to sleep, perhaps to dream.

Does that hen *lay* an egg every day?

**lie** *v.* 1. Recline; to rest. 2. Tell an untruth. *n.* An untruth.

Every afternoon, I *lie* down for a nap.

He appears honest, but appearances can *lie.*

One must not tell a *lie* to the F.B.I.

USAGE NOTE: Forms of *lay* and *lie* are often confused or used incorrectly. Examples of correct usage and common mistakes are listed below

.

| Correct | Incorrect |
| --- | --- |
| I shut the book and *laid* it down. | I shut the book and *lay* it down. |
| I decided to *lie* down after lunch. | I decided to *lay* down after lunch. |
| His is *lying* down on the job. | He is *laying* down on the job. |
| *Lie* low until the danger is past. | *Lay* low until the danger is past. |

 **Memory Tricks**

GRAMMAR: The verb **lay** always takes a direct object. You **lay** *something* down. The verb **lie** cannot take an object. You cannot **lie** something down.

GRAMMAR: Memorize the principal parts of the verbs **lay** and **lie:**

*Now* I **lay** it down. *Yesterday* I **laid** it down. I *have **laid** it down before.*

*Now* I **lie** down. *Yesterday* I **lay** down. I *have* **lain** down before.

115

# Try It!

Choose *lay* or *lie* for each ❑.
(See page 262 for answers.)

**1.** Who ❑ that wet washcloth on my wood table?

**2.** Yes, I cannot tell a ❑, but I did not mean to let the wet cloth ❑ there.

**3.** The husky ❑ down his bone and then ❑ down beside it.

**4.** I'll ❑ the towel on the sand so I can ❑ on it.

**5.** Before you ❑ down, ❑ the remote control on top of the TV.

**6.** She ❑ awake for hours, unable to sleep.

**7.** What danger ❑ around the corner?

**8.** You'd better ❑ down if you feel faint.

**9.** If you ❑ those scarves on the top shelf, they may ❑ there indefinitely before being sold.

**10.** If you are really willing to tell the truth, why are you unwilling to take a ❑ detector test?

**11.** Those piles of trash will ❑ along the street until they are collected.

# LEAD ... LED

 **Examples from Quotes**

Do not go where the path may **lead**; go instead where there is no path and leave a trail.
— *Ralph Waldo Emerson*

The mass of men **lead** lives of quiet desperation and go to the grave with the song still in them.
— *Henry David Thoreau*

If you do not choose to **lead,** you will forever be **led** by others. — *Michael Straczynski*

A great nation is not **led** by a man who simply repeats the talk of the street-corners or the opinions of the newspapers. — *Woodrow Wilson*

 **Dictionary Definitions**

**lead** *v.* To guide the way by going in advance. *n.* 1. A heavy, soft metal (rhymes with *dead.)* 2. A foremost position. 3. Material of possible use in a search.

Adele will *lead* the way to the cave.

My joke went over like a *lead* balloon.

An anonymous tip provided the detective with the *lead* she sought.

**led** *v.* Past tense and past particle of the verb "to *lead.*"

The tracks *led* from the cave to the river.

USAGE NOTE: The verb *led* (past tense) is often misspelled *l-e-a-d* because it is pronounced like its homonym *lead* (rhymes with *Ted*).

## Memory Tricks

RHYME: Think, "**Read** and you will take the **lead**."

RHYME: Think, "Ned **led** Ed, Ted, and Fred.

CONNECT: **lead** → **lead**er

Spelling: Both **lead** (rhymes with *bead*) and **led** follow spelling rules for vowel sounds. In **lead**, the vowel sound is long-*e* (*lead* rhymes with *bead*). **Led** has the short-e sound. (*Led* rhymes with *bed*.)

> RULES: When two vowels come together, the first is long, the second is silent ("the first does the talking, the second does the walking"): e.g., **lead**.
>
> When a vowel comes between two consonants, the vowel is short: e.g., **led**.

## Try It!

Choose *lead* or *led.* for each ❑.
(See page 263 for answers.)

**1.** We need someone who will take the ❑ and ❑ us back to the cabin.

**2.** If we had not been ❑ astray by moose tracks, we would be there by now.

**3.** Who's playing the male ❑ in the drama?

**4.** ❑ them to the nearest exit.

118

**5.** Which is the path that will ☐ us to the cave?

**6.** What are the symptoms of ☐ poisoning?

**7.** If we follow the river, it will ☐ us to the sea.

**8.** We need to find a new ☐ singer tonight because Rocque has laryngitis.

**9.** The value of that stock turned out to be less than we were ☐ to believe.

**10.** That one unfortunate mistake ☐ to the general's defeat.

**11.** Who will ☐ the team to victory?

**12.** Myles was chosen to ☐ the investigation into the mysterious death of Styles. In his capacity as Inspector, he had ☐ many investigations in the past. Did the ☐ pipe lying near the body ☐ him to suspect that Styles' death was no accident? Was it the dagger under the sofa? No, neither would have ☐ Myles to pronounce that it was death by poisoning. Rather, it was the faint smell of almonds in Styles' overturned glass that was the ☐ Myles needed. It ☐ him to suspect cyanide as the agent of death. That faint odor, similar to that of peach pits, ☐ to the eventual arrest of the murderer.

# LEAVE ... LET

 ## Examples from Quotes

For my part, I consider that it will be found much better by all parties to **leave** the past to history, especially as I propose to write that history myself.
— *Winston Churchill*

We should measure welfare's success by how many people **leave** welfare, not by how many are added.
— *Ronald Reagan*

I never **let** schooling interfere with my education.
— *Mark Twain*

Chance is always powerful. **Let** your hook always be cast; in the pool where you least expect it, there will be fish. — *Ovid*

 ## Dictionary Definitions

**leave** *v.* 1. To go out of or away from; depart. 2. To allow to remain. 3. To entrust; give to another to control.

We must *leave* now to escape the hurricane.

We can *leave* our valuables in the safe.

*Leave* it to George.

**let** *v.* 1. To give permission to; allow. 2. Used as an auxiliary verb in a command.

Is it all right to *let* the dog out?

Never *let* the puppy chew the rug.

*Let go* of the rope now.

USAGE NOTE: *Leave* is used incorrectly instead of *let* in commands such as *let go* and *let ...be*. The expressions *leave alone* and *let alone* are idiomatic and may be used interchangeably to mean "to refrain from bothering or interfering with."

 ## Memory Tricks

RHYME: I'll b**et** you'll **let** me g**et** a p**et**.

CONNECT: **leave** → *depart*. Think, "Don't **leave** without me. "Don't **leave** home without it."

CONNECT: **leave** → *entrust*. Think, "**Leave** it to *Beaver.*"

Spelling: Both **leave** and **let** follow spelling rules for vowel sounds. In **leave**, the vowel sound is long-*e* (**le͟ave** rhymes with *he͟ave*). **Let** has the short-*e* sound (**le͟t** rhymes with *be͟t*.) Rules: When two vowels come together, the first is long, the second is silent ("the first does the talking, the second does the walking"): **le͟ave**.

When a vowel comes between two consonants, the vowel is short: **le͟t**.

 ## Try It!

Choose *leave* or *let.* for each ☐.
(See page 263 for answers.)

**1.** Please ☐ me help you with that heavy package.

**2.** If we ☐ now, we'll beat the exit crowds.

**3.** We'll ☐ the question for now.

**4.** We need to ☐ early to catch our plane.

**5.** Are you willing to ☐ what happens to chance?

**6.** There is an old saying, "☐ sleeping dogs lie."

**7.** The hotel won't ☐ us check in until 2:00 P.M.

**8.** We may ☐ our baggage with them, however.

**9.** I hope I didn't ☐ my toothbrush at home.

**10.** If only I had ☐ the phone ring, I wouldn't have left it behind.

**11.** I don't suppose you'd ☐ me borrow yours?

**12.** Why did I even ask — except that I must have taken ☐ of my senses!

**13.** I always ☐ something behind.

**14.** I'll ☐ it all to you, Mr. Perfect!

**15.** Now ☐ me be. I want to sulk for a while.


**LESS** *See* **FEWER**

**LET** *See* **LEAVE**

**LIE** *See* **LAY**

# LIKE ... AS ... AS IF

 **Examples from Quotes**

Be **like** a duck. Calm on the surface, but paddling *like* the dickens underneath. — *Michael Caine*

Giving money and power to government is **like** giving whiskey and car keys to teenage boys.
— *P. J. O'Rourke*

*As* our enemies have found, we can reason **like** men, so now let us show them we can fight **like** men also. — *Thomas Jefferson*

Just **as** the soul sees but is not seen, so God sees but is not seen. — *Marcus Tullius Cicero*

Stop acting **as if** life were a rehearsal.
— *Wayne Dyer*

Work **as if** you were to live a hundred years. Pray **as if** you were to die tomorrow.
— *Benjamin Franklin*

 **Dictionary Definitions**

**like** *prep.* 1. Similar to. 2. In the same manner as.

She walks *like* an Egyptian.

**as** *conj.* 1. To the same extent that. 2. In the same manner.

She walks *as* an Egyptian walks.

**as if** *conj.* 1. In the same manner as; though.

> She walks *as if* she were an Egyptian.

USAGE NOTE: The common mistake is to use *like* instead of *as* or *as if. Like* is a preposition. It is followed by a noun or pronoun (the object of the preposition.) It is *not* followed by a verb. *As* and *as if* are conjunctions. They are followed by a subject (noun or pronoun) *plus* a verb.

CORRECT: Eat *like* a pig. Eat *as* a pig eats.

# Memory Tricks

GRAMMAR: **As** and **as if** take a verb; **like** does not.
CONNECT: Think, "Do **as** I say, not **as** I do."
CONNECT **like** → songs: "Mighty **Like** a Rose," '**Like** a Bridge Over Troubled Water," "Seems **Like** Old Times."

# Try It!

Choose *like, as,* or *as if* for each ☐.
(See page 264 for answers.)

**1.** Who was it who said, "Nothing spoils a party ☐ a genius"?

**2.** You look ☐ you've seen a ghost.

**3.** Was that remark meant ☐ a joke?

**4.** Don't talk to me ☐ I were a child.

**5.** It looks ☐ we might be in for some violent weather tomorrow.

**6.** He's ☐ busy ☐ he ever was.

**7.** I can't imagine why he thought he could hide a thing ☐ that from you.

**8.** Greg decided, ☐ Allen, to join the club.

**9.** They thought of themselves ☐ star-crossed lovers, ☐ Romeo and Juliet.

**10.** The girl in the photograph does look ☐ her.

**11.** Allison looks ☐ her mother.

**12.** ☐ I told you earlier, your test will be on Friday.

**13.** We need to hire more people ☐ you, ☐ you might have heard before.

**14.** ☐ they like to say, "There's no business ☐ show business!"

**15.** There's no time ☐ the present, is there?

**16.** They were late again, ☐ usual.

**17.** Joe blocks the linebacker ☐ a pro.

**18.** Is jealousy ☐ a green-eyed monster, ☐ William Shakespeare said?

**19.** That looks ☐ a diamond, but it might be a fake.

**20.** ☐ I was once told: If it fogs up ☐ a foggy mirror when you breathe on it for 2-4 seconds, it is not a diamond, but glass.

# LOOSE ... LOSE

## Examples from Quotes

Let **loose** the dogs of war.
— *Willam Shakespeare*, from *Julius Caesar*

I'm not concerned about all hell breaking **loose**, but that a *part* of hell will break **loose** . . . it'll be much harder to detect. — *George Carlin*

We didn't **lose** the game; we just ran out of time.
— *Vince Lombardi*

Never **lose** a holy curiosity. — *Albert Einstein*

## Dictionary Definitions

**loose** *adj.* Not fastened or secure; slack.

This belt is too *loose;* it needs tightening.

The elephant escaped from the zoo and is running *loose.*

**lose** *v.* 1. To mislay; be unable to find or keep. 2. To fail to win.

Did I *lose* my ring on the beach, or was it stolen?

Some games you win, some games you *lose*, and some are rained out.

USAGE NOTE: The common mistake is to spell *lose* with a double *o: loose.* This is because *lose* does not follow spelling rules. Logically, its vowel sound should be spelled *oo.*

126

# Memory Tricks

RHYME: The m**oose** slipped the n**oose** and is **loose.**
CONNECT: **lose** → **lost** to remember the single *o*.

# Try It!

Choose *loose* or *lose* for each ❑.
(See page 265- for answers.)

**1.** I hope you didn't ❑ the key to the safe.

**2.** The dog got ❑ because its collar was too ❑.

**3.** In the 1890's the invention of the safety bicycle—comfortable, fast, and with air-filled tires—was the Victorian woman's passport to ❑ the shackles of house and husband and ❑ herself in the joys of two-wheeling it, if only around town. To Victorians, who were so straight-laced that a ❑ woman was one who went without corsets, the bicycle was a threat that would tempt women to ❑ their frailty, femininity, and male-dependency — perhaps even their virtue. Victorian women took to bicycling like wild birds let ❑ from a cage take to flight. Despite heckling, jeers, and even stoning, they did not ❑ their zest for the sport. They did ❑ pounds of underwear and long, interfering skirts. In 1898 the Rational Dress Society approved seven pounds as the maximum weight of a woman's underclothing. Victorian fashion could not help but ❑ to the new "rational" fashion, exemplified by Bloomers (gasp!) and split skirts.

# MAY ... MIGHT

 ## Examples from Quotes

Your big opportunity **may** be right where you are now. — *Napoleon Hill*

Things **may** come to those who wait, but only the things left by those who hustle.
— *Abraham Lincoln*

Progress **might** have been all right once, but it has gone on too long. — *Ogden Nash*

There was another life I **might** have had, but I am having this one. — *Kazuo Ishiguro*

 ## Dictionary Definitions

**may** *v.* Auxiliary verb used to indicate possibility.

I *may* go to medical school and become a doctor.

**might** *v.* Past tense of auxiliary verb *may,* used to indicate possibility.

I *might* have become a doctor if I hadn't been drafted by the NFL.

USAGE NOTE: The difference in usage between *may* and *might* is one of degree and of time. *May* indicates a possibility. *Might* also indicates a possibility, but one that is not very likely. *Might* is also used to indicate a possibility that existed in the past: "I *might* (not *may}* have become a doctor."

# Memory Tricks

GRAMMAR: In general, don't use **may** to express a possibility that no longer exists.

RHYME: Last *night* I **might** have died of *fright*. To*day* I **may** just shout hoo**ray**!

 # Try It!

Choose *may* or *might* for each ☐.
(See page 266 for answers.)

**1.** My homework ☐ be in my locker, or a passing raven ☐ have flown off with it.

**2.** He ☐ have lived to be a hundred if only he had listened to me.

**3.** It ☐ be that hummingbirds find the color red especially attractive.

**4.** If the ball game hadn't been rained out, we ☐ have won.

**5.** Since Hurricane Elva ☐ arrive on Wednesday, it ☐ be a good idea to buy bottled water today.

**6.** I ☐ take a lunch break if we're not too busy.

**7.** I ☐ always win millions in the lottery — you never know!

**8.** I ☐ have gone to see that film, but I saw its bad reviews first.

**9.** Before long, humans ☐ vacation on Mars!

# NAVAL ... NAVEL

## Examples from Quotes

Because my father was often absent on **naval** duty, my mother suffered me to do much as I pleased.
— *John James Audubon*

Yesterday, December seventh, 1941, a date which will live in infamy, the United States of America was suddenly and deliberately attacked by **naval** and air forces of the Empire of Japan.
— *Franklin D. Roosevelt*

The ancient Greeks noticed that a man with arms and legs extended described a circle, with his **navel** as its center. — *Stephen Gardiner*

You can take all the sincerity in Hollywood, place it in the **navel** of a fruit fly and still have room for three caraway seeds and a producer's heart.
— *Fred Allen*

## Dictionary Definitions

**naval** *adj.* Of or pertaining to a navy.

During the war, there was a *naval* blockade of the harbor.

**navel** *n.* The depression in the middle of the abdomen of mammals where the umbilical cord was attached during gestation.

The pit at the top of a *navel* orange resembles a *navel*.

# Memory Tricks

CONNECT: **naval** → U.S. **Naval** Academy →**naval** base.

# Try It!

Choose *naval* or *navel* for each □.
(See page 266 for answers.)

**1.** The □ is the center of our physical bodies.

**2.** In 1776, England was a great □ power.

**3.** This □ telescope collapses to fit in a sailor's □.

**4.** If you are an omphalocentric, you practice contemplating your □ as an aid to meditation.

**5.** The battleship became the symbol of □ power and dominance.

**6.** A jewel adorned the belly-dancer's □.

**7.** The dockyard covers 50 acres and is used primarily for □ repairs.

**8.** She has received commission as a □ officer.

**9.** The sailors were all transferred to the American □ base at Guantanamo.

**10.** The statue was painted with elaborate designs from □ to foot.

**11.** Some say a large boulder on Easter Island in Chile is the "□ of the world."

# NOISOME ... NOISY

## Examples from Quotes

The body politic produces **noisome** and unseemly substance, among which are politicians.
— *P.J. O'Rourke*

The first flower to bloom in this latitude ... is not the fragrant arbutus, nor the delicate hepatica, nor the waxen bloodroot ... but the gross, uncouth, and **noisome** skunk cabbage. — *Alvan F. Sanborn*

The trouble with most comedians who try to do satire is that they are essentially brash, **noisy** and indelicate people who have to use a sledge hammer to smash a butterfly. — *Imogene Coca*

Our **noisy** years seem only moments in the being of the eternal silence. — *William Wordsworth*

## Dictionary Definitions

**noisome** *adj.* 1. Offensive to the senses (especially to the sense of smell). 2. Noxious, harmful.

The *noisome* fumes made us gag.

**noisy** *adj.* 1. Making noise. 2. Characterized by noise.

It's almost impossible to talk in this *noisy* cafeteria.

# Memory Tricks

ETYMOLOGY: **Noisome** comes from the same root as *annoy* and has no connection with *noise*. Think, *"annoy-some → **noisome**."*

 # Try It!

Choose *noisome* or *noisy* for each ❑.
(See page 267 for answers.)

**1.** At the ballgame, the ❑ yells of the fans assaulted my ears, while the ❑ aromas of sweat and sauerkraut offended my nose.

**2.** The room was so ❑ I couldn't hear myself think.

**3.** The ❑ aroma of *eau-de-skunk* dampened my enthusiasm for picnicking in the park.

**4.** The ❑ fumes arising from mixing chlorine and ammonia produce chlorine gas and can be fatal.

**5.** It is so ❑ in that nightclub that you can't hear the band, and the place reeks with the ❑ stale smell of tobacco.

**6.** A snake crawled out of the ❑, decaying swamp.

**7.** Some people prefer a ❑, congested city to the peace and quiet of the country.

**8.** As we approached the deserted cabin, a ❑ smell assailed our nostrils.

# OPHTHALMOLOGIST ... OPTICIAN OPTOMETRIST

 ## Examples from Quotes

**Ophthalmologists** are physicians who perform eye surgery, as well as diagnose and treat eye diseases and injuries. — U.S. Department of Labor, *Occupational Handbook*

Have your optical dive mask made by the **opticians** who invented them. — *James Cramer*

They don't take eyeballs at the bank. Those who value stocks by eyeballs should go be **ophthalmologists**, not stock analysts. — *Leonard Maggiore*

And **optometrists** get to do most of what **ophthalmologists** do, without the medical degree: diagnose and treat eye diseases, perform minor surgery (in some states), and of course fit people for glasses and contact lenses. — *Marty Nemko*

 ## Dictionary Definitions

**ophthalmologist** *n.* A physician who specializes in the structure and diseases of the eye.

The *ophthalmologist* removed the cataract.

**optician** *n.* One who makes and sells lenses, eyeglasses, and optical equipment.

This *optician* specializes in making prescription diving masks for people who wear glasses.

**optometrist** *n.* A health-care professional who examines the eye for visual defects and prescribes lenses or eye exercises.

The *optometrist* in the mall gives eye exams, prescribes lenses, and sells eyeglasses.

 **Memory Tricks**

CONNECT: **ophthalm<u>ologist</u>** → cardi<u>ologist</u>, dermat<u>ologist</u>, gastroenter<u>ologist</u>, onc<u>ologist</u> psycho<u>logist</u> (medical professionals).

CONNECT: **opti<u>cian</u>** → techn<u>ician</u> → beaut<u>ician</u> electr<u>ician</u> (hands-on occupations).

RHYME: Think,"If you don't need a doctor or pharmac<u>ist</u>, get your eyes checked by an **optometris<u>t</u>**. (An optometrist is not a doctor and can't prescribe medications.)

 **Try It!**

Choose *ophthalmologist, optician,* or *optometrist* for each ☐. (See page 267- for answers.)

**1.** Take this lens prescription to an ☐, who will be able to make prescription sunglasses for you.

**2.** The ☐ used laser surgery to repair the patient's torn retina,

135

**3.** My ☐ called in a prescription for eyedrops that treat cataracts in the hopes of avoiding cataract surgery.

**4.** An ☐ is not a physician but is, nevertheless, the main provider of such eye care as giving eye exams and diagnosing vision problems.

**5.** I'd take your eyeglasses to an ☐ to have that scratched lens replaced.

**6.** My local ☐ gave me an eye exam and offered a large assortment of eyeglass frames for me to choose from.

**7.** The ☐ routinely schedules operations to correct glaucoma on Wednesdays and Fridays.

**8.** You had better have your irritated eye checked by an ☐ to make sure you don't have an infection from contaminated contact lens solution.

**9.** I need to see an ☐ to get a new prescription for a pair of eyeglasses.

**10.** Eye injuries should be referred to an ☐ to ensure there is no infection.

**11.** Tracy took her young daughter to an ☐ to be fitted for glasses.

**12.** You need to be checked by an ☐ to make sure you don't have an eye infection.

# PASSED ... PAST

## Examples from Quotes

> Character is the ability to carry out a good resolution long after the excitement of the moment has **passed**. — *Cavett Robert*

> Any thought that is **passed** on to the subconscious often enough and convincingly enough is finally accepted. — *Robert Collier*

> Those who do not remember the **past** are condemned to relive it. — *George Santayana*

 ## Dictionary Definitions

**passed** v. Past tense and past participle of *to pass*. 1. To move beyond; to move past. 2. To transfer someone or something. 3. To be approved by a legislature.

> The speeding car *passed* us at 90 m.p.h.

> The quarterback *passed* the ball to the receiver.

> The bill *passed* the House but may not pass the Senate.

**past** *n*. The time before the present; time that has passed. *adj*. Over; having occurred before the present time. *prep*. Beyond.

> In the *past*, milk was delivered in bottles.

> In years *past*, milk was delivered in bottles.

> He went *past* the dairy aisle and stopped at produce.

USAGE NOTE: The common mistake is to use *past* as a verb instead of *passed. Past* is not a verb.
CORRECT: "We *passed* the church on our way to the library." "Midnight passed." INCORRECT: We *past* the church on our way to the library." "Midnight past."

 ## Memory Tricks

CONNECT: **passed** → action: "quarterback **passed** the ball."

CONNECT: **past** → time: Remembrance of things **past**.

CONNECT: **passed** → song lyrics: "My Future Just **Passed** By," "Love Has **Passed** Me By,"

RHYME: She was a**ghast** at the mention of her **past.**

RHYME: **Cass passed** on the **bass** and ate the steak.

 ## Try It!

Choose *passed* or *past* for each ☐.
(See page 268 for answers.)

**1.** Had she driven ☐ that same house sometime in the ☐ ?

**2.** A week had ☐ since he ☐ his driver's test, and still — no ticket!

**3.** In the ☐, the senator would have had no trouble having her resolution ☐, but now she was not so sure. Had her popularity ☐?

**4.** A month had ☐ since he had received her letter.

**5.** J.S. Bach □ on his musical ability to his son.

**6.** I think my electric bill is now □ due.

**7.** She accelerated and □ the tractor trailer.

**8.** A few moments □ before anyone spoke.

**9.** I'm afraid it's □ the deadline to enroll.

**10.** It is time for you to stop thinking about the □ and plan for your future.

**11.** She avoided his eyes as she walked □ him.

**12.** Suddenly a troubling thought □ through Vanessa's mind.

**13.** Had her □ indiscretions found her out and were they resurfacing?

**14.** So many years had □, and all that was in the □, wasn't it?

**15.** Surely Kyle wouldn't have □ her letters on to Lisle, would he?

**16.** That would be □ belief!

**17.** She had trusted Kyle completely in the □.

**18.** Had all his feeling for her now □?

**19.** The possibility that her □ lover had betrayed her was too much to face.

**20.** Vanessa felt her knees crumple beneath her, and she □ out.

# PRINCIPAL ... PRINCIPLE

## Examples from Quotes

The **principal** benefit acting has accorded me is the money to pay for my psychoanalysis.
— *Marlon* Brando

A mother is neither cocky, nor proud, because she knows the school **principal** may call at any minute to report that her child had just driven a motorcycle through the gymnasium. — *Mary Kay Blakely*

It is easier to fight for one's **principles** than to live up to them — *Alfred Adler*

I've distilled everything to one **principle:** win or die!
— *Glen Close*

## Dictionary Definitions

**principal** *adj.* 1. First; highest in rank. 2. Main; most important. *n.* 1. The person with controlling authority; the head of an organization. 2. Money on which interest it paid.

What are the *principal* reasons for our increase in sales?

The *principal* spoke at the teacher's meeting.

What is your monthly payment, including *principal* and interest?

**principle** *n.* A basic belief; fundamental standards.

The *principle* of equality underlies our justice system.

The right to free speech is a *principle* of democracy.

**Memory Tricks**

GRAMMAR: ***Principal*** can be either an adjective or a noun. ***Principle*** can only be a noun.

CONNECT: Think: The ***principal*** is my **pal.**

CONNECT the ***a* in principa̲l** with the ***a* in ma̲in.**

CONNECT the ***ciple*** in ***principle*** with the ***ciple*** in *disciple.* Think, "*Disciples* spread ***principles*** they believe in."

 **Try It!**

Choose *principal* or *principle* for each ☐.
(See page 269 for answers.)

**1.** What is your ☐ reason for deciding to resign?

**2.** The school ☐ believed that the ☐ of free speech did not give students the right to openly insult teachers.

**3.** What is the difference between following the ☐ of the law and following the "letter of the law"?

**4.** It may be the ☐ of gravity that is the ☐ cause of wrinkles and sagging skin attributed to age.

**5.** The irrational ☐ upon which your argument is based is my ☐ objection to it.

# PRONE ... SUPINE

## Examples from Quotes

Moon! Moon! I am **prone** before you. — *Amy Lowell*

One of my fondest memories of the chief is watching him lying **prone** on floor of his house, pretending to shoot a rifle. — *Ted Cruz*

There is no calamity which a great nation can invite which equals that which follows a **supine** submission to wrong and injustice.
— *Grover Cleveland*

He was hailed by a **supine** press as the second coming of Lincoln at Cooper Union.
— *Charles Krauthammer*

## Dictionary Definitions

**prone** *adj.* 1. Lying face downward; prostrate. 2. Tending; inclined.

Lying *prone,* she crawled under the barbed wire.

She is *prone* to be impetuous and takes unnecessary chances.

**supine** *adj.* 1. Lying on the back with face upward. 2. Apathetic; not inclined towards action.

Lying *supine,* he gazed at the stars.

Benjamin Franklin said that those who are on guard against their adversaries are in much less danger of being attacked than the *supine.*

USAGE NOTE: It is the primary meanings of *prone* and *supine* that are apt to be confused: "lying face downward" and "lying face upward," respectively. *Supine* is often used in a figurative sense; that is, someone lying supine is in a defenseless position and, hence, not inclined toward action, passive.

 ## Memory Tricks

CONNECT: **prone** → **pro**strate → lying on your **p**aunch.

CONNECT: **supine** → lying on your **spine**.

 ## Try It!

Choose *prone* or *supine* for each ❏.
(See page 269- for answers.)

**1.** She assumed a ❏ position to do push-ups.

**2.** I am ❏ to sleep on my back, ❏.

**3.** He lay down on the weight bench ❏ and raised the weights above his head.

**4.** Harry is ❏ to be ❏, that is, to take the path of least effort and resistance.

**5.** If you lie ❏, it will be it easier to find your contact lens on the floor.

**6.** They lay ❏, watching for falling stars.

**7.** Being overtired makes him ❏ to errors.

# QUALIFY ... QUANTIFY

## Examples of Quotes

I was appalled at the amount of study necessary in order to **qualify** in medicine, and gradually my desire was blunted by a keener—and secret—wish to become an actor. — *Conrad Veidt*

At the heart of personality is the need to feel a sense of being lovable without having to **qualify** for that acceptance. — *Paul Tournier*

It is now possible to **quantify** people's levels of happiness pretty accurately by asking them, by observation, and by measuring electrical activity in the brain, in degrees from terrible pain to sublime joy. — *Polly Toynbee*

## Dictionary Definitions

**qualify** *v.* 1. To meet the requirements of. 2. To make more specific or modify.

What are the requirements to *qualify* for a student loan?

Let me *qualify* my remark.

**quantify** *v.* 1. To determine the quantity of. 2. To measure and express as a number.

We will identify and *quantify* the qualities leading to financial success.

Can you *quantify* the results of your study?

## Memory Tricks

CONNECT: **qualify** → **qualif**ication → **quali**ties.

CONNECT: **quantify** → **quanti**ty → **quant**um.

## Try It!

Choose *qualify* or *quantify* for each ☐.
(See page 270 for answers.)

**1.** How can one give a number to, or ☐, the impact and relevance of this research?

**2.** The number of years it takes for babies' names to rise and then fall in popularity helps us to ☐ how long fads last.

**3.** What must I do in order to ☐ as a contestant on your TV game show?

**4.** We conducted the survey to ☐ the effects of our new advertising campaign.

**5.** It is not possible to ☐, or put a measure to, the value of love or of friendship or of loyalty.

**6.** How can I find out if I ☐ for disability benefits?

**7.** To ☐ for membership in Mensa International you need only score in the top 2% of the population on an approved intelligence test.

**8.** Is an intelligence test, such as the Stanford-Binet, a reliable means to ☐ intelligence?

### QUAY *See* KEY

# REIGN ... REIN

## Examples from Quotes

God is the only being who, in order to **reign**, doesn't even need to exist. — *Charles Baudelaire*

The painter must give a completely free **rein** to any feeling or sensations he may have and reject nothing in which he is naturally drawn.
— *Lucian Freud*

Ignorant free speech often works against the speaker. That is one of several reasons why it must be given **rein** instead of suppressed.
— *Anna Quindlen*

## Dictionary Definitions

**reign** *n.* 1. The rule of a sovereign, such as a king. 2. The period of time in which a sovereign rules. *v.* To exercise sovereign power.

Shakespeare lived during the *reign* of Queen Elizabeth I.

The king was to *reign* for over fifty years.

**rein** *n.* 1. A long strap attached to a bit held in an animal's mouth and used to control the animal. 2. A restraint. *v.* To control or restrain.

Pull, don't jerk, the *rein*.
You need to *rein* in that horse.

# Memory Tricks

CONNECT: **reign** → king →regal → sove**reign**.
CONNECT: **rein** → the expression "**rein** in."

# Try It!

Choose *reign* or *rein(s)* for each ❑.
(See page 270 for answers.)

**1.** She pulled back on the ❑, trying to get control of the horse, but could not ❑ him in.

**2.** How long do you think his ❑ as world champion will last?

**3.** Peace would ❑ for forty-seven years during the ❑ of the pharaoh.

**4.** She was given free ❑ to do whatever she thought necessary to save the company.

**5.** He gave his horse the ❑ and galloped to the finish line.

**6.** In the third year of her ❑ there was a revolt.

**7.** What will it take to make him ❑ in his temper?

**8.** To start up a canter from a walk, pull up on the curb ❑ a little and turn the head slightly right.

**9.** The teacher managed the horse with a leading ❑ until he could entrust his pupil with the ❑.

**10.** The two rulers could no longer ❑ together.

**11.** During the ❑ of King George III, Parliament made attempts to ❑ in the rebellious American colonists, without success.

**12.** In 1776, during the ☐ of Louis XVI of France, Benjamin Franklin charmed the French court and won a sizable loan for the American army.

**13.** The hapless King Charles II was to ☐ over England in what was arguably its worst year in history, 1666, the year of the great fire of London, in which 80% of the city burned down.

**14.** This ☐ of fire raged for five days, and even months afterwards, small fires continued to burn throughout the city.

**15.** Frantic attempts to ☐ in the fire were futile.

**16.** The catastrophe did, however, succeed in putting an end to the ☐ of the city's vast rat population.

**17.** So many rats and their resident fleas perished in the blaze, that it effectively put an end to the ☐ of the Black Death, or Great Plague, in that beleaguered city.

**18.** Afterwards, officials were kept busy trying to ☐ in citizens trying to lynch French catholic extremists (whom they blamed for the fire, whose real cause was sparks from the oven of the King's royal baker).

# RESTFUL ... RESTIVE

 **Examples from Quotes**

A cat pours his body on the floor like water. It is **restful** just to see him. — *William Lyon Phelps*

What makes a river so **restful** to people is that it doesn't' have any doubt — it is sure to get where it is going, and it doesn't want to go anywhere else. — *Hal Boyle*

Once a man has tasted creative action, then thereafter, no matter how safely he schools himself in patience, he is **restive**, acutely dissatisfied with anything else. — *Jean Toomer*

It is a hard although a common case. To find our children running **restive**—they in whom our brightest days we would retrace. — *Lord Byron*

 **Dictionary Definitions**

**restful** *adj.* 1. Providing for tranquility. 2. At rest, tranquil.

The boat's gentle rocking was soothing and *restful.*

**restive** *adj.* Restless under control; fidgety.

The audience grew *restive* as the speaker droned on.

# Memory Tricks

WORD PARTS: **restful** = "full of **rest**."

TONGUE TWISTER: ***Restive,*** *restless reckless rebels refuse to relax.*

# Try It!

Choose *restful* or *restive* for each ☐.
(See page 271 for answers.)

**1.** Cruising down the river on a Sunday afternoon can be a relaxing, ☐ experience for some, but can make those of a more restless, impatient disposition ☐ and irritable.

**2.** Concerned that the prisoners were growing ☐, prison authorities tried piping in soothing, ☐ music.

**3.** When the weather prevented children from going outside for recess, they became increasingly ☐ and difficult to teach.

**4.** Green and blue are ☐ colors, but when their walls are painted screaming pink or flamboyant orange, residents become ☐.

**5.** After supervising rambunctious third-graders on a trip to the zoo, I looked forward to the ☐ calm of my quiet apartment.

**6.** Her horse was getting ☐ and pawed the ground.

**7.** Let's spend a ☐ day in the country.

# SET ... SIT

## Examples from Quotes

**Set** the foot down with distrust on the crust of the world — it is thin. — *Edna St. Vincent Millay*

Words mean more than what is **set** down on paper. — *Maya Angelou*

I don't care where I **sit** as long as I get fed. — *Calvin Trillin*

Humorists always **sit** at the children's table. — *Woody Allen*

## Dictionary Definitions

**set** *v.* To put or place (something)

*Set* the groceries on the counter.

**sit** *v.* 1. To rest with the buttocks or hindquarters resting on a supporting surface. 2. To be located or situated.

I'll *sit* on the couch.

The packages *sit* on the floor by the door.

USAGE NOTE: *Set* is a transitive verb. It takes a direct object. You *set* (put or place) something somewhere. *Sit* is an intransitive verb. It does not take a direct object. *Sit* is not an action you do to an object (whether the object be animate or inanimate.) The common error is to use *set* as an

151

intransitive verb meaning "*sit.*" <u>CORRECT</u>: "*Sit* in the chair next to me." <u>INCORRECT</u>: "*Set* in the chair next to me."

 ## Memory Tricks

Connect: **sit** → "**Sit,** Rover.  Good dog!"

*Connect:* **sit** → "**Sit** up straight

*Connect:* **set** → "**Set** the table." (**Set** silverware and dishes on the table.)

 ## Try It!

Choose *set* or *sit* for each ☐.
(See page 272 for answers.)

**1.** Make sure all the troublemakers ☐ in the first row, where you can see them, and never let Mark ☐ next to Dennis!

**2.** Be very careful when you ☐ down that liquid.

**3.** Just ☐ your books on the counter and ☐ down.

**4.** If you ☐ your package on the floor, someone will be able to ☐ in that seat.

**5.** If you ☐ the TV on the kitchen shelf, we'll be able to ☐ and watch it as we eat.

# SHALL ... WILL

 ## Examples from Quotes

I hope I **shall** always possess firmness and virtue enough to maintain what I consider the most enviable of all titles, the character of an "Honest Man." — *George Washington*

Never, never, and never again **shall** it be that this beautiful land will again experience the oppression of one by another. — *Nelson Mandela*

Experience is the best teacher, but a fool **will** learn from no other. — *Benjamin Franklin*

No longer **shall** I paint indoors with men reading and women knitting. I **will** paint living people who breathe and feel and suffer and love.
— *Edvard Munch*

 ## Dictionary Definitions

**shall** *v.* 1. In the first person *(I* or *we)* expresses futurity. 2. In the second or third person, expresses (a) determination, resolve; (b) inevitability; (c) must.

> We *shall* finish the project tomorrow.
>
> You *shall* do it now, or else!

**will** *v.* 1. Formal usage: in the second or third person, expresses futurity. 2. In the first person, expresses (a) determination, resolve; (b) inevitability; (c) must.

You *will* receive the package tomorrow.

I *will* do this, even if I do nothing else!

USAGE NOTE: The distinction between *shall* and *will* is rapidly disappearing. *Will* has been used to express futurity in the first, second, and third persons by renowned writers. In speaking and informal writing, the use of the contractions of *shall* and *will* makes a choice unnecessary. For occasions when formal usage is indicated, however, it is wise to observe the formal usage "rules." The *shall/will* rules reverse to show determination rather than futurity. To show determination, first person uses *will.* Second and third person use *shall* to show determination.

     **Memory Tricks**

CONNECT: **shall** → *the song "Shall* we dance?" (1st person, future tense).

REPETITION: Think, "**Will** Will have the *will* to win?" (3rd person, future tense).

     **Try It!**

Choose *shall* or *will* for each ☐. (See page 272 for answers.)

**1.** We ☐ go to the cabin tomorrow if you ☐ agree to meet us there.

**2.** No, I absolutely ☐ not do what you ask, and never mention it again!

**3.** They ☐ follow the regulations or I'll see them in court!

**4.** He ☐ arrive in New York at 6:30.

**5.** I ☐ not go to Los Angeles, and there's no way you can make me; I ☐ think about a trip to Las Vegas, however.

**6.** They said they ☐ be here in time for supper.

**7.** We ☐ be at the exit in ten minutes.

**8.** I certainly ☐ leave to join the circus, no matter how much you object!

**9.** You ☐ turn down that music, if you know what's good for you!

**10.** If it is meant to be, it ☐ be.

**11.** ☐ we go now during the intermission, or would you prefer to stay?

**12.** I'm busy right now, but I ☐ have time to meet with you tomorrow afternoon.

**13.** Believe me, he ☐ be punished for his crime!

**14.** You ☐ do it, if you know what's good for you!

**15.** What ☐ we do if it rains?

**16.** It ☐ be disastrous if we miss our flight!

**17.** Where ☐ we eat tonight?

### SIT *See* SET

# STATIONARY ... STATIONERY

## Examples from Quotes

Moreover, since the sun remains **stationary**, whatever appears as a motion of the sun is really due rather to the motion of the earth.
— *Nicolaus Copernicus*

When people shake their heads because we are living in a restless age, ask them how they would like to live in a **stationary** one and do without change. — *George Bernard Shaw*

A logo should look as good in 15-foot letters on top of company headquarters as it does one sixteenth of an inch tall on company **stationery**.
— *Steven Gilliatt*

He sent anniversary and birthday cards on Cowboys' **stationery**. He turned most into Cowboys fans. — *Mack Brown*

## Dictionary Definitions

**stationary** *adj.* In a fixed position; unmoving.

The gym has ten *stationary* bikes for cardio workouts.

A *stationary* storm front has settled over the area.

**stationery** *n.* Writing paper; office supplies.

The *stationery* supplies I need include inkjet paper, file folders, and tape.

## Memory Tricks

CONNECT: **stationary** → st_a_nd, st_a_y, st_a_tic ("a" spelling = "unmoving").

CONNECT: **stationery** → l_e_tt_e_r, pen.

## Try It!

Choose *stationary* or *stationery* for each ☐.
(See page 273- for answers.)

**1.** Now that I've named my company, I must design ☐ and business cards.

**2.** As a musician, I constantly traveled, but now I finally have a ☐ home next to a ☐ store.

**3.** I understand, however, that the ☐ store is about to move—if a ☐ store can move, that is.

**4.** During the earthquake, ☐, coffee cups, and pens flew off the desk, which remained ☐, since it was bolted to the floor.

**5.** Her beliefs never ever wavered and were as unmovable and ☐ as the giant and noble trees she vowed to protect.

**6.** "Never, never will I buy ☐ made from any but recycled paper!" she vowed.

## SYMPATHY See EMPATHY

## TAKE *See* BRING

# THAN ... THEN

## Examples from Quotes

Few things are harder to put up with **than** a good example. — *Mark Twain*

It is easier to forgive an enemy **than** to forgive a friend. — *William Blake*

To thine own self be true, and it must follow, as the night the day, thou canst not **then** be false to any man. — *William Shakespeare*

I wake up every morning at nine and grab the morning paper. **Then** I look at the obituary page. If my name is not on it, I get up.
— *Benjamin Franklin*

## Dictionary Definitions

**than** *conj.* Introduces the second part of a comparison.

> Wine is sweeter *than* vinegar.

> My brother is taller *than* I. (taller *than* I am tall)

**then** *adv.* 1. At that time in the past. 2. Next in a series or order. 3. At another time in the future.

> I once lived in that house, but that was *then;* now is now.

> First preheat the oven, and *then* bake the pizza.

> One day I'll be discovered by Hollywood, and *then* life will be perfect!

USAGE NOTE: A common mistake is to use the wrong pronoun after *than*. To avoid this problem mentally supply the missing verb. CORRECT: She walks faster *than* he (. . . faster *than* he walks). INCORRECT: She walks faster *than* him (. . . faster *than* him walks).

 ## Memory Tricks

CONNECT: **th<u>a</u>n** → comp<u>a</u>re (both contain an *a*).
CONNECT: **th<u>e</u>n** → n<u>e</u>xt (both contain an *e*).

 ## Try It!

Choose *than* or *then* for each ☐.
(See page 273 for answers.)

**1.** He seems to think he is better ☐ anyone else.

**2.** Less ☐ a month later, another hurricane struck.

**3.** Just ☐ a stranger came running through the woods towards them.

**4.** Are you better off ☐ you were a year ago?

**5.** We can't go back for your vitamins because ☐ we would miss the train.

**6.** I was an accountant, but since ☐ I have left my job and become a self-published author.

**7.** Of all romances in history, few were more tempestuous ☐ that of Napoleon Bonaparte and Josephine.

**8.** Napoleon had never been more smitten ☐ when he met the beautiful Paris socialite, a widow, who was ☐ thirty-two years old.

**9.** Josephine at first evaded his advances, but ☐ relented, and they were married in 1796.

**10.** Napoleon ☐ went on military campaigns.

**11.** Rather ☐ˋbrood over his absence, Josephine ☐ attended to her own affairs, adulterous though they were.

**12.** On hearing about her conduct, the enraged Napoleon ☐ demanded a divorce.

**13.** But when Josephine pleaded with him, he ended up forgiving, rather ☐ divorcing, her.

**14.** They did not ☐ live happily ever after, for when Napoleon became emperor, he divorced Josephine, hoping for a son.

**15.** He married a woman who was much younger ☐ Josephine and who did ☐ bear him a son.

**16.** Josephine died while Napoleon was in exile; he ☐ escaped and returned to Paris.

**17.** The grief-stricken Napoleon ☐ picked violets from Josephine's garden and put them in a locket, which he ☐ wore until his death.

**18.** Napoleon loved no woman more ☐ Josephine.

## THAT *See* WHO

# THEIR ... THERE ... THEY'RE

 ## Examples from Quotes

Forgive your enemies, but never forget **their** names.
— *John F. Kennedy*

Even if you're on the right track, you'll get run over if you just sit **there**. — *Will Rogers*

Nobody goes **there** anymore. It's too crowded.
— *Yogi Berra*

Maybe if you can't get somebody out of your head, **they're** supposed to be **there**.
— *Unknown*

 ## Dictionary Definitions

**their** *adj.* Possessive form of the pronoun *they;* shows possession.

If the fence is *their* property line, it is *their* fence.

**there** *adv.* 1. In or at that place. 2. Used to begin a sentence, has no meaning of its own.

Y our keys are *there*, on the counter.

*There* are leaves on the golf course, but my ball is in the clear over *there*.

**they're** Contraction of *they are.*

The Johnsons say *they're* going to move to Florida.

# Memory Tricks

CONNECT: **their** → **heir**. "I am **their heir."** (An *heir* will own something. **Their** shows ownership.)

CONNECT: **there** → **here**. Think, "It's neither **here** nor **there**."

WRITE: Write out a row of the word **they're**, but in place of each apostrophe, write a tiny *a*: **they^are, they^are, they^are, they^are.** Read each aloud as *they are*. Then repeat the procedure, reading each aloud as **they're**.

# Try It!

Choose *their, there,* or *they're* for each ☐.
(See page 274 for answers.)

**1.** ☐ on ☐ way and should be here soon.

**2.** ☐ are only a few who disagreed with ☐ decision.

**3.** Is that ☐ dog over ☐ by the barn?

**4.** If ☐ sure they put ☐ lunch ☐ on the picnic table, what became of it?

**5.** ☐ claiming that is not ☐ baseball over ☐ by the broken window.

**6.** ☐ are millions of Monopoly® fans worldwide, but ☐ largely unaware that ☐ favorite board game helped Allied POWs escape from Nazi prison camps thanks to the British Secret Service and ☐ Operation Monopoly.

**7.** The Brits had a company making silk escape maps carried by ☐ airmen.

**8.** The factory-made Monopoly® games ☐, as well.

**9.** Maps and Monopoly® — ☐ unlikely candidates to be paired in a secret service plot. Not so.

**10.** ☐ plan was to hide escape maps and tools inside the game boxes and smuggle them into German prison camps along with Red Cross packages sent ☐.

**11.** They marked ☐ "special edition" games with a red dot in the FREE PARKING space.

**12.** ☐ boxes were altered with carefully cut holes and slots.

**13.** ☐ were extra playing pieces: a file, compass, and silk escape map specific to the region and showing the "safe houses."

**14.** ☐ was real foreign currency to be used as bribes under the Monopoly® money.

**15.** To be compliant with the Geneva Convention, the Nazis distributed Red Cross packages and the Monopoly® games to ☐ prisoners.

**16.** Some 35,000 Allied prisoners escaped German prison camps. How many owed ☐ escape to the game of Monopoly®?

**THEN** *See* **THAN**

163

# TO ... TOO ... TWO

## Examples from Quotes

A very quiet and tasteful way **to** be famous is **to** have a famous relative. — *P. J. O'Rourke*

I do a couple of hundred press-ups a day but I haven't been **to** a gym in years. — *Simon Cowell*

There are a number of things wrong with Washington. One of them is that everyone is **too** far from home. — *Dwight D. Eisenhower*

Outside of a dog, a book is a man's best friend. Inside of a dog it's **too** dark to read.
— *Groucho Marx*

To succeed in life, you need **two** things: ignorance and confidence. — *Mark Twain*

Three can keep a secret, if **two** of them are dead.
— *Benjamin Franklin*

## Dictionary Definitions

**to** Used before a verb to indicate the infinitive: *to go; to think. prep.* 1. Suggesting movement toward something. 2. Relation to.

I don't have *to* answer your questions.

Does this bus go *to* Albuquerque?

**too** *adv.* 1. In addition to; also. 2. To an excessive degree.

> Not only is that hat *too* expensive, but the shoes are *too!*

**two** *n.* The number written as 2; one more than one in number.

> *Two* are company and three's a crowd.

 ## Memory Tricks

GRAMMAR*:* **To** is always followed by another word; it cannot end a sentence. In an infinitive (verb form), it is followed by a verb: **to** *go.* As a preposition, it is followed by a noun or pronoun: **to** *Joe;* **to** *them.*

CONNECT: **too** → **too** *many.* **To** and **too** are frequently confused. To remember that **too** means "excessive," think, "**Too** has **too** many *o*'s. It has one extra *o.*"

CONNECT*:* **two** → **tw**in, **tw**elve, **tw**enty, **tw**ice.

 ## Try It!

Choose *to, too,* or *two* for each ❑.
(See page 276 for answers.)

**1.** Did you ever feel ❑ tired ❑ go ❑ bed?

**2.** I received ❑ dollars ❑ much in change.

**3.** I only had ❑ hours of sleep — far ❑ little.

**4.** ❑ desserts are ❑ ❑ many for me!

**5.** Let's go ☐ Texas ☐ by ☐.

**6.** Elvis Presley was no stranger ☐ guns.

**7.** In 1970 Elvis went ☐ the White House unannounced ☐ petition Richard Nixon ☐ appoint him as an undercover agent.

**8.** He wanted ☐ investigate drug abuse and Communist brainwashing techniques ☐.

**9.** Elvis went prepared. He packed ☐ handguns, one for himself, the other ☐ give ☐ Nixon, who might need protection, ☐.

**10.** Not ☐ be outdone, Nixon gave a gift ☐ Presley — a Special Assistant badge from the Bureau of Narcotics and Dangerous Drugs.

**11.** The FBI got into the act, ☐, and gave Presley permits ☐ carry firearms in every state ☐ assist him in pursuing his undercover work.

**12** Elvis kept his firearms readily available at home in Graceland, ☐.

**13.** He was known ☐ shoot his TV set whenever Mel Torme came on the screen.

**14.** He accorded this treatment to Robert Goulet, ☐, when Goulet appeared on TV.

**15.** Elvis's car, ☐, fell victim ☐ his gun-toting temper.

**16.** When his car refused ☐ start, he shot it.

# UNDO ... UNDUE

## Examples from Quotes

A reformer knows neither how to do nor to **undo**.
— Jose *Bergamin*

You can't **undo** the past . . . but you can certainly not repeat it. — *Bruce Willis*

It is worthwhile too to warn the teacher that **undue** severity in correcting faults is liable at times to discourage a boy's mind from effort. — *Quintilian*

There is no road too long to the man who advances deliberately and without **undue** haste; there are no honors too distant to the man who prepares himself for them with patience. — *Jean de la Bruyere*

## Dictionary Definitions

**undo** *v.* 1. To reverse or erase. 2. To untie or unwrap.

The computer has a button that enables you to *undo* the last thing you typed on your screen.

**undue** *adj.* 1. Excessive. 2. Not just or legal. 3. Not due.

We all worry about our problems, but *undue* worry doesn't solve anything and, in fact, adds to our problems.

## Memory Tricks

WORD PARTS: **un-** + **do**. **Undo** = "to do the reverse."

WORD PARTS: **un** + **due**. **Undue** = "not due" (e.g., **undue** praise is praise that is "not due." It is excessive praise.

## Try It!

Choose undo or undue for each ☐.
(See page 276 for answers.)

**1.** I regret the ☐ harshness of my remarks and wish I could ☐ them.

**2.** Although it is not possible to ☐ the actions of the past, it is possible to give them ☐ attention.

**3.** It is not possible to ☐ the knots in this tangled mass of marionette strings without spending ☐ time and effort.

**4.** If only it were possible to ☐ my actions.

**5.** Please help your little brother ☐ his shoelaces.

**6.** It was not possible to ☐ what he had done without ☐ expense and effort.

**7.** Be careful about appearing over-eager or of showing ☐ enthusiasm because you will run the risk of seeming unsophisticated.

**8.** If you change your attitude and henceforth refrain from ☐ criticism of your partner, you can ☐ the damage done to your relationship.

## UNINTERESTED See DISINTERESTED

# VAIN ... VEIN

## Examples from Quotes

The finest words in the world are only **vain** sounds if you cannot comprehend them.
— *Anatole France*

He does not live in **vain** who employs his wealth, his thought, and his speech to advance the good of others.
— *Hindu Proverb*

I have seen the movement of the sinews of the sky and the blood coursing in the **veins** of the moon.
— *Allama Iqbal*

Seas were meant to be sailed by those with salt in their **veins** and love in their hearts.
— *Anthony T. Hincks*

 ## Dictionary Definitions

**vain** *adj.* 1. Unsuccessful, futile. 2. Without worth or substance. 3. Exhibiting excessive pride in one's appearance or accomplishments.

The rescue attempt was in *vain*.

He went on a grapefruit and water diet in a *vain* attempt to lose weight.

She is so *vain* that she takes every remark as a compliment.

**vein** *n.* 1. A blood vessel in which blood travels to the heart. 2. A long strip or crack. 3. A turn of attitude or mood.

If you cut a *vein,* it does not spurt blood as an artery does.

In this locality, a *vein* of quartz may contain flecks of gold.

 **Memory Tricks**

RHYME: So **vain**, to look on others with dis**dain**. Much better to be a br**ain** or pl**ain**.

CONNECT: **vein** → blood **ve**ssel.

 **Try It!**

Choose *vain* or *vein* for each ☐. (See page 277 for answers.)

**1.** Those are ☐ promises, without substance.

**2.** The prospectors struck a ☐ of silver.

**3.** In a more serious ☐, here are the latest figures on inflation.

**4.** Alvin's three previous attempts to pass his driver's test were in ☐.

**5.** The nurse drew blood from a ☐ in his left arm.

**6.** Although quite beautiful, she was not ☐ about her appearance.

# WAS ... WERE

## Examples from Quotes

If we knew what it **was** we **were** doing, it would not be called research, would it? — *Albert Einstein*

I remember the time I **was** kidnapped and they sent a piece of my finger to my father. He said he wanted more proof. — *Rodney Dangerfield*

If I **were** two-faced would I be wearing this one? — *Abraham Lincoln*

If all economists **were** laid end to end, they would not reach a conclusion. — *George Bernard Shaw*

## Dictionary Definitions

**was** *v.* Past tense of the verb *to be,* 1st and 3rd person singular.

I'm sorry I *was* late, but he *was* late, too.

**were** *v.* 1. Past tense of the verb *to be,* all plurals and 2nd person singular. 2. Subjunctive of the verb *to be* (indicates a condition "contrary to fact").

What *were* we thinking when we invited him!

If only I *were* sixteen again. I wish I *were.*

USAGE NOTE: The most common mistake using *was* is to use it after the wrong pronoun. *Was* is used only after the pronouns *I, he, she,* and *it* (i.e., the 1st and 3rd person singular pronouns). It is never used after *you* (2nd person pronoun). It is never used after *we* or *they* (plural pronouns).

171

CORRECT: *I was* late yesterday. *He was* late yesterday. *She was* late yesterday. *It was* late yesterday.

INCORRECT: *You was* late yesterday. *We was* late yesterday. *They was* late yesterday.
　　To sum up: Never say or write: *you was* , *we was*, or *they was*.

*Were,* on the other hand, is used after *we, you, and they* to express past tense of the verb *to be.*
　　CORRECT: *We were* late yesterday. *You were* late yesterday. *They were* late yesterday.
*Were* has another use, however. It is used to indicate that a statement is *hypothetical* (may or may not be true); or that it is a *condition contrary to fact* (is not a fact).
　　HYPOTHETICAL: IF I *were* rich, I'd be happy.
　　CONTRARY TO FACT: If wishes *were* horses, beggars would ride. (Wishes are not horses; it's a condition contrary to fact.)

Clue words for the use of *were* include: *if, I wish, would, as, as if,* and *though.*

 **Memory Tricks**

SONGS: To remember that "*you **were**" is correct (not "*you was*") think of the song titles "You **Were** Always on My Mind" and "Wish You **Were** Here."

# Try It!

Choose *was* or *were* for each ☐.
(See page 277 for answers.)

**1.** She ☐ surprised to see there ☐ only a few customers in the diner.

**2.** If I ☐ you, I would order a salad instead.

**3.** I think it ☐ Robin Williams who said, "If you ☐ right, I'd agree with you."

**4.** When you ☐ in Hoboken, I ☐ in Hackensack.

**5.** It ☐ fate. You and I ☐ in the right place, and it ☐ the right time.

**6.** You ☐ gorgeous and I ☐ rich.

**7.** Together we ☐ perfect.

**8.** What ☐ it the poet wrote . . . something about if paradise ☐ now?

**9.** Oh, if only I ☐ a poet and my words ☐ poems!

**10.** Whether we ☐ fools or dreamer matters not.

**11.** We ☐ in love. Or, if it ☐ not love, it ☐ something quite like it.

**12.** ☐ it to last? Alas, life is not perfect. If only it ☐!

173

# WEATHER ... WHETHER

 ## Examples from Quotes

Climate is what we expect, **weather** is what we get.
— *Mark Twain*

We will act consistently with our view of who we truly are, **whether** that view is accurate or not.
— *Tony Robbins*

It's not **whether** you get knocked down, it's **whether** you get up. — *Vince Lombardi*

 ## Dictionary Definitions

**weather** *n.* 1. The state of atmospheric conditions. 2. Disagreeable atmospheric conditions. *v.* To endure unfavorable conditions.

The *weather* forecast said "scattered showers."

She was determined to *weather* the latest family crisis.

**whether** *conj.* 1. If it is the case that. 2. Used to introduce an option or alternative.

Please find out *whether* the museum is open.

It is immaterial to me *whether* we go to Reno or Rio.

 ## Memory Tricks

PRONUNCIATION: The common mistake is to spell **whether** like **weather** because *whether* is often mispronounced so that the two words sound the same. The **wh** in *whether* is pronounced like the **wh** in **wh**ere: Both words begin with the same sound. Practice repeating **wh**ere, **whether** until the correct pronunciation of **whether** sounds right to you.

ALLITERATION: Practice saying the following sentence aloud, paying special attention to the **wh**'s: **Whether** or not _Wh_itney drinks _wh_isky or _wh_atever is of no importance to me.

## Try It!

Choose _weather_ or _whether_ for each ☐.
(See page 278 for answers.)

**1.** I don't know ☐ to wash the car today or wait until the ☐ cooperates.

**2.** Grit your teeth and ☐ the storm, ☐ or not you're frightened.

**3.** No matter ☐ it rains, sleets, or snows, you know you'll have ☐.

**4.** They say Los Angeles never has ☐, but I don't know ☐ or not I agree with that.

**5.** It doesn't matter ☐ the ☐ is good or bad, everybody talks about it.

**WELL** See **GOOD**

**WERE** See **WAS**

**WHICH** See **WHO**

# WHO ... WHICH ... THAT

 **Examples from Quotes**

A friend is one **who** knows you and loves you just the same. — *Elbert Hubbard*

Nonviolence, **which** is a quality of the heart, cannot come by an appeal to the brain.
— *Mahatma Gandhi*

Any society **that** would give up a little liberty to gain a little security will deserve neither and lose both. — *Benjamin Franklin*

 **Dictionary Definitions**

**who** 1. Interrogative pronoun: *Who?* 2. Relative pronoun: the person or persons that.

Hilda, *who* is my cousin, goes to the University of Iowa.

**which** Relative pronoun in a nonrestrictive clause (one that gives additional information that is non--essential and could be left out).

I turned on WBIR, *which* is my favorite channel. (non-essential clause)

**that** Relative pronoun in a restrictive clause (one that is essential to sentence meaning).

Is this the face *that* launched a thousand ships? (essential clause).

USAGE NOTE: *Who* (or *whom*) refers to people. *Which* refers to animals or things and begins a clause that gives non-essential information.

 ## Memory Tricks

CONNECT: To remember that *who* refers to a person, think, "*Who's who?*"

GRAMMAR: To choose between *which* and *that,* drop the clause the word introduces from the sentence. If the sentence sense is unchanged, choose *which.* If not, choose *that.*

 ## Try It!

Choose *who, which,* or *that* for each ☐.
(See page 278 for answers.)

**1.** I wonder ☐ planted the daffodils ☐ have sprung up along the barnyard fence.

**2.** I used to live in Talbott, ☐ is a small town in East Tennessee.

**3.** One of my friends in our local book club recommended ☐ historical novel to me.

**4.** Joan found a realtor ☐ helped her sell her house, ☐ was a brick rancher ☐ had a heated pool.

**5.** Claude is the only one ☐ could have known what happened on ☐ fateful day.

**6.** Judo is not an activity ☐ one usually associates with presidents.

**7.** Yet our 26th president, ☐ was Theodore Roosevelt, was a judo enthusiast.

**8.** Theodore Roosevelt earned a distinction ☐ was unique, one ☐ few have ever heard about.

**9.** He was America's first Brown Belt in Judo, ☐ is a sport of unarmed combat ☐ was derived from jujitsu.

**10.** Roosevelt practiced judo in the White House basement, ☐ he covered with training mats.

**11.** He practiced judo with anyone ☐ was available, including his wife and sister-in-law.

**12.** Once during an official White House lunch, ☐ was unsurprisingly boring, he threw the visiting Swiss minister to the floor and demonstrated a hold ☐ he learned in judo.

**13.** This boisterous activity was a diversion ☐ delighted his other guests, although probably not the one ☐ brushed himself off as he got up from the floor.

**14.** The president's popularity, ☐ was great, was bolstered further when he went hunting in Mississippi and refused to shoot a black bear cub.

**15.** This story, ☐ touched America's heart, had an interesting result.

**16.** People began naming their stuffed toy bears "Teddy," ☐ is a name ☐ has stuck.

# WHO ... WHOM

## Examples from Quotes

A man **who** has no imagination has no wings.
— *Mohammad Ali*

Nothing is impossible for the man **who** doesn't have to do it himself. — *A. H. Weiler*

Have I reached the person to **whom** I am speaking?
— *Lily Tomlin as "Ernestine"*

Tell me **whom** you love, and I'll tell you **who** you are. — *Creole Proverb*

## Dictionary Definitions

**who** 1. Interrogative pronoun: *Who?* 2. Relative pronoun: the person or persons that.

**whom** *pro.* The objective case of *who* (object of a verb or preposition).

*Who* stole the plans?

Sebastian is the spy *who* stole the plans.

He is the spy *whom* our agent contacted.

He is the one to *whom* we gave false information.

USAGE NOTE: *Who* is always the subject of a verb. *Whom* is always the object of a verb or a preposition. The mistake considered most objectionable is using *who* after a preposition (e.g., "the man to *who*").

# Memory Tricks

SUBSTITUTION: To check on the usage of **who**, see if it could refer to the subject pronoun *he, she,* or *they.* EXAMPLE: "spy **who** stole our plans"; "*he* stole our plans."

SUBSTITUTION: To check on the usage of **whom**, see if it could refer to the object pronoun *him, her,* or *them.* EXAMPLE: "**whom** our agent contacted"; "our agent contacted *him.*"

## Try It!

Choose *who* or *whom* for each ☐.
(See page 279 for answers.)

**1.** Did you see ☐ left the package at the door?

**2.** To ☐ is the package addressed, and ☐ is the sender?

**3.** Ralph, ☐ first noticed the suspicious package, is not one ☐ is easily rattled. He is, however, someone ☐ easily leaps to false conclusions, and to ☐ a number of false alarms in the form of 911 calls have been attributed. Perhaps this is only to be expected from one ☐ devours spy novels and tales of espionage. He is a person for ☐ I have the utmost respec and ☐ I hold in deepest regard. Yet Ralph is someone ☐ prefers to live life as fiction, someone ☐ likes to believe that behind every occurrence lurks a spy.

# WHO'S ... WHOSE

## Examples from Quotes

You're not the only one **who's** made mistakes, but they're the only things that you can truly call your own. — *Billy Joel*

I like a man **who's** good, but not too good—for the good die young, and I hate a dead one. — *Mae West*

Never go to a doctor **whose** office plants have died. — *Erma Bombeck*

I have friends in overalls **whose** friendship I would not swap for the favor of the kings of the world. — *Thomas A. Edison*

## Dictionary Definitions

**who's** Contraction of *who is* or *who has.*

Who's on first base? *(who is)*

Who's been sitting in my chair? *(who has)*

**whose** The possessive form of *who.*

Whose book is this?

Whose side are you on?

## Memory Tricks

WRITE: Write a row of the word ***who's***, but in place of each apostrophe, write a tiny *i*: ***whoⁱs, whoⁱs, whoⁱs, whoⁱs***. Read each aloud as *who is* and then as *who's*. Repeat the procedure, this time

181

substituting **ha** for the apostrophe and reading each aloud as *who has* and then as *who's.*

REPLACE: If you are unsure whether *who's* or *whose* is correct in a sentence, replace the *who's/whose* word with *who is.* If the sentence makes sense, write *who's.* If not, write *whose.*

## Try It!

Choose *who's* or *whose* for each ❑.
(See page 280 for answers.)

**1.** ❑ the teacher ❑ been the most influential in your life?

**2.** It was Mr. Gillespie, ❑ words inspired me and ❑ always been a role model for me.

**3.** He's one of those people ❑ face is familiar but ❑ name escapes me.

**4.** ❑ the author of that book about Captain Ahab, ❑ nemesis is a giant white whale?

**5.** ❑ got a suggestion on a good book to read at the beach?

**6.** I want one ❑ plot is thrilling, a real page-turner.

# YOUR ... YOU'RE

## Examples from Quotes

> The best way to make **your** dreams come true is to wake up! — *J.M. Power*
>
> If **you're** not making mistakes, then **you're** not doing anything. — *John Wooden*
>
> **You're** only as good as **your** last haircut.
> — *Fran Lebowitz*
>
> You know **you're** old if **your** walker has an airbag.
> — Phyllis Diller

## Dictionary Definitions

**your** adj. The possessive form of the pronoun *you*.

> This is *your* lucky day! *Your* ticket has the winning number.

**you're** Contraction of *you are*.

> *You're* not going to believe this, but *you're* the winner!

USAGE NOTE: *Your/you're* are frequently confused because they sound alike and both appear to be possessives. Although an apostrophe signals possession in nouns, pronouns have their own possessive forms. *Your* is the possessive form of *you*, not *you're*.

# Memory Tricks

CONNECT: **your** → **our**. The word **your** has the smaller word *our* in it. Both are pronouns that show possession. ("**your** family," "*our* family")

- WRITE: Write out a row of the word **you're**, but in place of each apostrophe, write a tiny *a*: **you$^a$re, you$^a$re, you$^a$re, you$^a$re**. Read each aloud as *you are* and then as **you're**.

# Try It

Choose *your* or *you're* for each ❑.
(See page 280 for answers.)

**1.** Let a smile be ❑ umbrella on a rainy day; for when ❑ smiling, the whole world smiles with you.

**2.** What is that song ❑ singing?

**3.** Is that song, "❑ No One If ❑ Not on Twitter"? Or is it, "If ❑ Happy and You Know It, Clap ❑ Hands"?

**4.** I guess ❑ tone deaf. Actually, I was singing, "❑ Going to Get ❑ Fingers Burnt."

**5.** That song is my second favorite song after "❑ So Vain."

**6.** If ❑ tastes run to Country Western, try, "When You Leave, Walk Out Backwards So I'll Think ❑ Walking In."

**7.** Or you might like one of these: "You Can't Have ❑ Kate and ❑ Edith Too," or "My John Deere

184

Was Breaking ☐ Field, While ☐ Dear John Was Breaking My Heart."

**8.** If you like those, I'd recommend, "Am I Double Parked by the Curbstone of ☐ Heart?"

**9.** One of my all-time favorites is: "You Changed ☐ Name from Brown to Jones and Mine from Brown to Blue."

## ZEALOUS *See* JEALOUS

# Words
# Commonly
# Misused

# Conquer 50 Words Commonly Misused

Are you guilty of word misuse? Most of us are from time to time. We misuse a word when we think we know what it means but really don't. Unknowingly, we use it with a mistaken meaning — and may continue to do so for years. Where do these mistaken meanings come from? Often, they come from others. When a word is commonly misused, its misuse begins to sound and look right. Thus, its misuse is passed on. Usage errors are easy to perpetrate — somewhat like a virus.

Fortunately, such usage errors are easy to correct. Usually all it takes is to become aware of them. In light of that, the chart that follows explains the real meanings of 50 commonly misused words. Acquaint yourself with them and you will be ahead of the game — one of the few who know how to use them correctly and what they really mean.

| | |
|---|---|
| **ACCESS** | Mistakenly used to mean "an amount beyond what is needed, an excess." |
| | **INCORRECT:** There is a charge for *access* baggage. |
| | *Access* means "the right to enter or make use of; a means of entering, passage." |
| | **CORRECT:** You do not have the legal right to *access* those documents. |

**ADVERSE**

Mistakenly used to mean "opposed to; reluctant, *averse.*"

INCORRECT: I am not *adverse* to exercise.

*Adverse* means "hostile to; unfavorable."

CORRECT: The playwright was stung by the critic's *adverse* comments.

**ALIBI**

Mistakenly used to mean "an excuse."

INCORRECT: What is your *alibi* for being late?

*Alibi* means "a defense plea of having been elsewhere when an act was committed."

CORRECT: What *alibi* did Higgins give for where he was the night of the crime?

**ALTERCATION**

Mistakenly used to mean "a physical fight."

INCORRECT: An *altercation* broke out between demonstrators and onlookers.

*Altercation* means "a noisy quarrel, a dispute."

CORRECT: Our conversation was interrupted by a noisy *altercation* between the waiter and a patron.

| | |
|---|---|
| **AMBIVALENT** | Mistakenly used to mean, "I don't care one way or another." |
| | **INCORRECT**: I'm *ambivalent* about which film to see. Either one is fine. |
| | *Ambivalent* means "having mutually conflicting thoughts or feelings." |
| | **CORRECT**: His *ambivalent* feelings about marriage prevented him from popping the question. |
| **ANXIOUS** | Mistakenly used to mean "eager." |
| | **INCORRECT**: I'm so *anxious* to see my new grandson! |
| | *Anxious* means "to be uneasy or apprehensive, worried." |
| | **CORRECT**: Sylvia grew *anxious* as her turn to speak grew closer. |
| **BI-** versus **SEMI-** *(weekly, monthly, annual)* | The prefix *bi-* means "two" or "every two." The prefix *semi-* means "half" or "twice." When these prefixes begin a word referring to a period of time, however, they can cause misunderstanding. *Bi-*, for example, has acquired a nonstandard meaning that is used frequently. Instead of meaning "twice" it can now also mean "every two." Thus, *biweekly* can be interpreted as "twice a week" or "every two weeks." Confusing? Undoubtedly. In order to avoid confusion, it is often better to reword your message in order to make your meaning clear. For instance, if you mean "every two weeks," |

say so rather than using the words *biweekly* or *semimonthly*.

Here's a summary of usage:

*Biweekly* means "every two weeks." **NONSTANDARD:** "twice a week" or "semiweekly." *Bimonthly* means "every two months." **NONSTANDARD:** "twice a month" or "semimonthly." *Biyearly* means "every two years." **NONSTANDARD:** "twice a year," "semiyearly."

But ... *biannual* means" twice a year," or" semiannual." *Biennial* means" lasting two years," "occurring every two years." *Semiweekly* means "twice a week." *Semimonthly* means "twice a month." *Semiannual* means "twice a year."

**COMPARE**

In formal usage, *compare* is used to note likenesses. *Contrast* is used to note differences.

<u>INCORRECT</u>: If you *compare* apples and oranges, you will find some striking differences between them.

In informal usage only, *compare with* may be used to note similarities or differences. But it is incorrect to use *compare to* in that way.

**COMPENDIOUS**

Mistakenly used to mean "very lengthy; encyclopedic."

INCORRECT: Albertson's *compendious,* unabridged, Hungarian dictionary weighs over five pounds.

*Compendious* means "concise, terse, abridged."

CORRECT: This short, *compendious* U.S. history devotes one paragraph to the 1930s dust bowl.

**CONSEQUENT**

Mistakenly used to mean "subsequent."

INCORRECT: After his first novel his *consequent* works were disappointing.

*Consequent* means "following as a natural event or result." *Subsequent* means "following in time or order; succeeding."

CORRECT: The use of pesticides and *consequent* damage to the environment is a matter of grave concern.

**DENOTE**

Mistakenly used to mean "connote; to suggest or imply."

INCORRECT: To me, the word "home" *denotes* a place of rest, love, and comfort.

*Denote* means "to indicate; to refer to specifically."

CORRECT: A fever may *denote* an infection.

| | |
|---|---|
| **DIFFUSE** | Mistakenly used to mean "defuse to reduce danger or tension." |

**INCORRECT:** He customarily used humor to *diffuse* tension in the workplace.

*Diffuse* means "to disperse."

**CORRECT:** Use this spray-atomizer to *diffuse* the scent throughout the room.

| | |
|---|---|
| **DOWNGRADE** | Mistakenly used to mean "denigrate — to defame, slander, insult, or belittle." |

**INCORRECT:** The candidate sought to *downgrade* her opponent's reputation.

*Downgrade* means "to lower the status or value of."

**CORRECT:** The municipal bonds were *downgraded.*

| | |
|---|---|
| **DUE TO** | Mistakenly used to introduce an adverbial phrase that gives the reason for or cause of the action of the main verb. |

**INCORRECT:** D*ue to* construction delays on Route 44, we arrived late.
Acceptable alternatives: *because of, through, on account of, owing to.*

*Due to* functions as a predicate adjective after a linking verb (verb "to be") and means "because of."

**CORRECT:** Her indecision was *due to* a lack of a definite purpose.

| ECONOMIC | Mistakenly used to mean "not wasteful; thrifty, economical." |
|---|---|
| | **INCORRECT:** Having an *economic* nature, he is always turning off lights. |
| | *Economic* means "relating to the economy, or large-scale finances." |
| | **CORRECT:** What are the first signs of an *economic* recovery? |
| ENERVATE | Mistakenly used to mean "energize." |
| | **INCORRECT:** I take a brisk walk before breakfast to *enervate* me and make me alert. |
| | *Enervate* means "to drain of energy, to weaken." |
| | **CORRECT:** The heat and humidity of the tropics combined to *enervate* us and rob us of initiative. |
| ENORMITY | Mistakenly used to mean "enormousness, immensity." |
| | **INCORRECT:** We were overwhelmed by the *enormity* of the Colosseum. |
| | *Enormity* means "outside moral boundaries, heinous on a huge scale, excessive wickedness." |
| | **CORRECT:** The enormity of the regime's crimes was beyond belief. |

**ETC.**

Mistakenly used to refer to people.

INCORRECT: The course is of benefit to writers, speakers, students, etc.

*Etc.* means "and so forth; and the rest." It is used at the end of a list of things, not of people.

CORRECT: Bring any kind of dessert, such as cheesecake, apple pie, English trifle, Bavarian cream, etc.

**FLUKE**

Mistakenly used to mean "a stroke of bad news."

*Fluke* always refers to a stroke of good luck or a fortunate chance event. It originally referred to a lucky stroke in billiards.

**GOURMAND**

Mistakenly used to mean a gourmet, one who appreciates fine food and drink.

INCORRECT: You won't go wrong letting Herb choose the restaurant. He's a *gourmand.*

A *gourmand* is someone who eats to excess, a glutton.

CORRECT: It was repugnant to watch the *gourmand* stuff himself with food.

**INFAMOUS**

Mistakenly used to mean "famous."

INCORRECT: The highly esteemed actor rose from being a rodeo rider to an honored celebrity with an *infamous* reputation.

*Infamous* means "having a bad reputation, detestable."

CORRECT: The identity of the *infamous* serial killer Jack the Ripper remains unknown.

**INGENUOUS**

Mistakenly use to mean "intelligent, clever, ingenious."

INCORRECT: What a clever invention, and how *ingenuous* of you to have thought of it!

*Ingenuous* means "candid, naive, not sophisticated."

CORRECT: The *ingenuous* young man did not realize that the frank expression of his opinion was not appropriate.

**IRONIC**

Mistakenly used to mean "an amusing coincidence."

INCORRECT: How *ironic* that we have the same birthday!

*Ironic* means "an outcome opposite from the expected outcome; an intended meaning opposite to the literal meaning."

CORRECT: How *ironic* that he spent his life trying to achieve fame, yet it was his death that made him famous.

**LIMPID**

Mistakenly used to mean "limp, frail."

INCORRECT: The *limpid* wilted daffodils drooped loosely over the edge of the vase.

*Limpid* means "transparently clear; easily intelligible."

CORRECT: The pure and *limpid* stream has its source in the mountains.

**LITERALLY**

Mistakenly used to mean "practically."

INCORRECT: The children were *literally bursting* with anticipation.

*Literally* means "actually, without exaggeration."

CORRECT:  He *literally* does not know how to boil an egg.

**MITIGATE**

Mistakenly used for *militate,* which means "to have an effect against; to counteract."

**INCORRECT:** The proposed amendment *mitigates* against free speech.

*Mitigate* means "to moderate; to make less bad."

**CORRECT:** The lawyer pleaded *mitigating* circumstances to reduce his client's sentence.

| | |
|---|---|
| **MORBID** | Mistakenly used to mean "sad, unpleasant." |

**INCORRECT:** His *morbid* disposition is his only companion.

*Morbid* means "diseased, unhealthy in mind and body."

**CORRECT:** He is mentally unstable and has a *morbid* fascination with death.

| | |
|---|---|
| **MUTE** | Mistakenly used to mean "open to debate, debatable, as in a 'moot' point." |

**INCORRECT:** Arguing about whether to go to the mountains or the beach is a *mute* point, since we can't afford to go on a vacation.

*Mute* means "refraining from or being unable to speak."

**Correct:** I couldn't hear the video because I had mistakenly hit the *mute* button.

| | |
|---|---|
| **NEMESIS** | Mistakenly used to mean merely "an enemy, a hostile person." |

**INCORRECT:** I'm always tripping over that cat. She's my *nemesis*.

*Nemesis* is a much stronger word than *enemy*. It is "an avenging force." In classical mythology Nemesis was the goddess of retribution. She punished both excessive pride and wrongdoing and came to represent retributive justice or revenge. In sports, a *nemesis* is an unbeatable rival.

**CORRECT:** Superman's arch *nemesis* is Lex Luthor, just as Batman's is the Joker.

**NONPLUSSED**

Mistakenly used to mean "cool, calm and collected."

**incorrect:** *Nonplussed* by his tirade, she calmly walked out the door.

*Nonplussed* means "perplexed, baffled, bewildered."

**CORRECT:** *Nonplussed* by her remark, he wondered, "What does she mean by that?"

**ODIOUS**

Mistakenly used to mean "detectable by smell, odorous, or odiferous.

**INCORRECT:** I was repulsed by the *odious* smell of stale cigar smoke.

*Odious* has no connection with the word *odor*. It means "hateful, abhorrent, offensive."

**CORRECT:** With a sigh, he began the *odious* task of correcting exam papers.

**OFFICIOUS**

Mistakenly used to mean "like an officer."

INCORRECT: He handled the task admirably in an *officious* and commanding manner.

*Officious* has nothing to do with the words *officer* or *official*. It means "aggressively nosy, meddlesome, excessively forward in offering service or advice."

CORRECT: My landlord is an *officious* busybody who is always barging in with unwanted suggestions and offers of assistance.

**PEACEABLE**

Mistakenly used to mean "serene, calm, peaceful."

INCORRECT: I love to retreat to this quiet *peaceable* spot by the lake.

*Peaceable* means "inclined to avoid strife; disposed toward peace."

CORRECT: In one of Edward Hick's *Peaceable Kingdom* paintings, William Penn is shown concluding a *peaceable* treaty with the Native Americans.

**PENULTIMATE**

Mistakenly used to mean "ultimate."

INCORRECT: This resort spa is absolutely fabulous, the *penultimate* in luxury.

*Penultimate* means "the next to last."

CORRECT: This is the fourth, or *penultimate*, concert in the series of five, which will conclude on January 25.

**PERUSE**

Mistakenly used to mean "to look over casually; to glance over quickly."

INCORRECT: I *perused* the book quickly and decided it was not for me.

*Peruse* means "to read or examine thoroughly with great care."

CORRECT: *Peruse* this report carefully to ensure there are no ambiguous statements or inaccuracies.

**PLETHORA**

Mistakenly used to mean "a lot, many."

INCORRECT: The newly married couple was welcomed by a *plethora* of well-wishers.

*Plethora* means "overabundance, an excess." It often carries a negative connotation.

CORRECT: The bill needs to pass through a *plethora* of committees and subcommittees before being considered for a vote.

**PRACTICABLE**

Mistakenly used to mean "relating to practice rather than theory; practical."

INCORRECT: The book is a straightforward, *practicable* guide to finding an apartment in New York City.

*Practicable* means "possible, capable of being done or used."

CORRECT: Although constructing a bridge over the Strait of Messina may be *practicable*, the immense cost involved probably makes it impractical.

**PRECEDENCE**

Mistakenly used to mean "an act or instance that may be used to judge subsequent incidences; a precedent."

INCORRECT: This law decision might set a dangerous *precedence*.

*Precedence* means "to go before; take priority."

CORRECT: Those arriving first will be given *precedence* for seating.

**PRISTINE**

Mistakenly used to mean "spotless; as good as new."

INCORRECT: The carpet was spotless, a *pristine* white.

*Pristine* means "pertaining to the earliest time or condition; in a state virtually unchanged from the original."

CORRECT: The gold coins they recovered were *pristine*, in newly minted condition.

**PROGENITOR**

Mistakenly used to man "inventor."

INCORRECT: Thomas A. Edison was the *progenitor* of the lightbulb.

Progenitor *means "direct ancestor."*

CORRECT: President John A. Adams was the *progenitor* of a distinguished family, including his son President John Quincy Adams.

| QUAY | Mistakenly used to mean "an offshore island, a key." |
|---|---|

**INCORRECT:** We beached our boat on an uninhabited *quay* five miles from the mainland.

*Quay* (pronounced like *key*) means "a wharf or landing place built parallel to a waterway to unload ships."

**CORRECT:** We walked down the wide cement *quay,* which was alongside the riverbank.

| RANDOM | Mistakenly used to mean "spontaneous; someone living in an irregular and unrestrained way." |
|---|---|

**INCORRECT:** She is an impetuous, *random* person.

*Random* means "having no specific pattern; chance, arbitrary."

**CORRECT:** The winning ticket number will be selected at random from all the tickets sold.

| REDUNDANT | Mistakenly used to mean "useless or unable to perform or function." |
|---|---|

**INCORRECT:** When is Riley going to admit that he's *redundant*, that it's time for him to retire?

*Redundant* means "superfluous, needlessly repetitive."

**CORRECT:** In the phrase "last will and testament," the word "testament" is *redundant* because it means "last will."

**RESTIVE**

Mistakenly used to mean "restful, conducive to rest."

INCORRECT: Unfortunately, our vacation was not *restive* because of the noisy children in the next room.

"*Restive* means "impatient, stubborn, restless, agitated."

CORRECT: The audience grew *restive* waiting for the rock concert to start.

**RETICENT**

Mistakenly used to mean "reluctant."

INCORRECT: He is *reticent* to commit himself to a relationship.

*Reticent* means "be silent, reserved, taciturn."

CORRECT: He is never *reticent* when asked to express his opinion of rap music.

**SEASONABLE**

Mistakenly used to mean "relating to or dependent on a season, seasonal."

INCORRECT: Jobs in the amusement park are *seasonable.*

*Seasonable* means "timely, appropriate to the season."

CORRECT: This cool weather will be gone by *Wednesday* and will become more *seasonable* for July.

**TANTAMOUNT**

Mistakenly used to mean "best, the top, paramount."

**INCORRECT:** This committee's *tantamount* concern is to arrive at the truth.

*Tantamount* means "equal to in effect or value."

**CORRECT:** To say you don't recall what the committee discussed and concluded is *tantamount* to admitting your incompetence.

**UNDO**

Mistakenly used to mean," excessive, not just, undue."

**INCORRECT:** If your job causes *undo* stress, why don't you quit?

*Undo* means "to reverse or erase, to untie or unstrap."

**CORRECT:** If only I could *undo* the injury I have done you!

**VERSE**

In formal usage, *verse* is mistakenly used to mean "a poem or stanza (division of) a poem."

I finally memorized that entire *verse* on Hiawatha by Longfellow.

*Verse means "a line of poetry."*

**CORRECT:** The poem consists of three stanzas, with four verses in each stanza.

**WRONGFUL**

**INCORRECT:** We made a *wrongful* turn and got lost.

*Wrongful* means "unjust, unfair; not sanctioned by law."

**CORRECT:** Did circumstantial evidence lead to her *wrongful* conviction for the crime?

# No-No's in Your Speech and Writing

escape goat

# Eliminate 25 No-No's From Your Speech & Writing

No-No's are mistakes. They occur so often that in many cases they have come to sound and look correct. It's easy to use them yourself, but don't be misled. Those in the know frown on such words and phrases because they are incorrect either grammatically or lexically (relating to vocabulary).

No-no's include nonexistent words (e.g., *alright*), incorrect idiomatic expressions (e.g., *could care less*), incorrect idiomatic use of prepositions (e.g., *could of*), nonstandard usage or meanings (e.g., *ignorant* to mean "rude"), and words with built-in redundancies (e.g., *reiterate*). I selected the no-no's in this chapter because they are common errors and are frequently listed in style guides and usage manuals. They are listed in a table to make them easy to access.

Begin by scanning the entries on the following pages to discover which you need to study. Undoubtedly, you will recognize some entries as known errors, but others may give you pause. "Is that an error? I didn't realize that." Since the list is a manageable size, a brief scan will quickly tell you what you need to learn. All of the errors listed occur frequently in speech and writing.

Be one of the few who knows your *no-no's* and refuses to use them. Show your superior word savvy. Purge the following offenders from your speech and your writing.

| | |
|---|---|
| **ALOT** | Not a word. Instead, use two separate words: *a lot*.<br><br>*A lot* means "a large number or amount; to a great degree or extent."<br><br>**A lot** of people write the words **a lot** incorrectly as one word. |
| **ALRIGHT** | Not a word. Write it as two words: ***all right***. Because ***all right*** is commonly said as one word, it is mistakenly written that way, as well.<br><br>***All right*** means "very well, okay, without a doubt."<br><br>After the storm, we checked the property to make sure everything was **all right**. |
| **ANYWAYS** | ***Anyways*** was an acceptable word in Middle English, but it has outlived its usefulness and acceptability. Avoid ***anyways*** and replace it with ***anyway***. ***Anyway*** is an adverb, and adverbs are plural. Thus it cannot end in the *s*-plural.<br><br>***Anyway*** means "regardless, in any event, in any manner whatever, nevertheless."<br><br>I know I probably won't win, but I intend to enter the contest **anyway**. |

**BEG THE QUESTION**    This expression is mistakenly used to mean "raise the question or bring up the question."

INCORRECT: The rapidly rising rate of juvenile delinquency **begs the question**, "What is happening to our parents?

To *beg the question* means to present as true or taken for granted a premise that needs proof—i.e., it means assuming as true what needs to be proved (otherwise known as a "circular argument").

Example of begging the question.

The reason the film star's outrageous story deserves nationwide media coverage is obvious: Look at it, it's everywhere. (Fallacy: It assumes as true that the reason it deserves coverage is because it gets coverage.)

**BURSTED**    This is an incorrect form of the verb *to burst* (whose principal parts are: *burst, burst, burst.)* In other words, there is no such word as **bursted.** Use **burst** instead. *(INCORRECT: The child winced as the balloon **bursted.**)*

CORRECT: The child winced as the balloon **burst.**

**COULD CARE LESS**    The correct phrase is *could not care less* or *couldn't care less.*

INCORRECT: I *could care less* about ice hockey. (Illogical. It means that the speaker cares about ice hockey but possibly could care less about it.)

CORRECT: I am not at all interested in ice hockey and **couldn't care less** about it.

| COULD OF | The correct expression is **could have,** not **could of.** (INCORRECT: I **could of** danced all night!) |
| | CORRECT: I **could have** danced all night. |

| DILIGENCY | Not a word. Instead, use **diligence.** |
| | INCORRECT: He applied himself to the task with **diligency.** |
| | *Diligency* means "persistent effort; long, steady application to work or study." |
| | CORRECT: He applied himself to the task with **diligence.** |

| ESCAPE GOAT | The correct word is *scapegoat.* Its origin traces back to an ancient rite on the Hebrew Day of Atonement when the high priest lay the sins of the people on the head of a goat. The goat was then taken into the wilderness to carry away the sins of the people. (Perhaps the original word did mean "escape goat," since the goat escaped into the wilderness and also escaped being sacrificed.) |
| | *Scapegoat* means a person, often innocent, on whom blame is heaped or punishment inflicted for something someone else has done. In the vernacular, a *scapegoat* is a "fall guy." |

Although innocent, he became the **scapegoat** because they needed someone to blame.

**FASTLY**

Not a word.

INCORRECT: With the holidays **fastly** approaching, I'd better start shopping.

CORRECT: With the holidays **fast** approaching, I'd better start shopping.

**FINAL ULTIMATUM**

This phrase is redundant since *ultimatum* encompasses the meaning "final." Use *ultimatum* by itself, without a modifier.

*Ultimatum* means "a final statement of terms; one's last word on a subject."

Rejection of our **ultimatum** may lead to the severing of diplomatic relations.

**FOR ALL INTENSIVE PURPOSES**

The correct phrase is *for all intents and purposes*.

*For all intents and purposes* means "for all practical purposes; in effect."

These unsold items from our garage sale are, **for all intents and purposes,** useless.

211

| | |
|---|---|
| **HEARTWRENCHING** | Not a word. It may have originated by mistakenly connecting it to the similar word *gut-wrenching*. The correct word is **heartrending.** |
| | *Heartrending* means, "inciting anguish, arousing deep sympathy; extremely moving." |
| | The Derby opened with a **heartrending** rendition of "My Old Kentucky Home." |
| **HAVE YOUR CAKE AND EAT IT TOO** | INCORRECT. The correct expression is: *You can't have your cake and eat it too.* |
| **HONE IN ON** | INCORRECT. The correct phrase is *home in on*. |
| | *Home in on* means "to aim at a target" (as a homing pigeon aims at its home). In contrast, *to hone* means "to sharpen" (as you would *hone* a blade to sharpen it.) |
| | Police are **homing in on** the robbery suspect. |
| **IGNORANT, MEANING "RUDE"** | Mistakenly used to mean "rude" rather than "uneducated, not knowledgeable." |
| | Although initially **ignorant** of official protocol, she learned quickly. |
| **IRREGARDLESS** | Not a standard word. Instead, use *regardless.* |
| | *Regardless* means "in spite of; without regard for." |
| | I must have that ring **regardless** of its cost. |
| **NAUSEOUS** | Mistakenly used to mean **nauseated.** |
| | INCORRECT: I feel **nauseous**. CORRECT: I feel **nauseated.** |

*Nauseous* means "causing or able to cause nausea."

The **nauseous** odor made me feel sick.

| | |
|---|---|
| **ORIENTATED** | <u>INCORRECT</u>. The correct word is *oriented*. |
| | *Oriented* means "aligned in position with reference to another point." |
| | The architect **oriented** the entrance to face south. |
| **QUICKER** | There is *quick and quickly,* but no such word as *quicker.* Instead, use *faster.* |
| **REITERATE** | Avoid using this word. Purists object to it on the grounds that it is redundant. Since *iterate* means "to say again, to repeat," the *re* prefix, meaning "again" is a redundancy. |
| **REOCCURRENCE** | Not a word. Instead, use *recurrence.* |
| | *Recurrence* means "to *occur* again; to return to one's memory." |
| | Fortunately, once the leak was fixed, there was no **recurrence** of the problem. |
| **SCOTCH** | Mistakenly used as an adjective to refer to a person or object from Scotland. (<u>INCORRECT</u>: *Angus MacPherson is Scotch.*) |
| | Use the following words to refer to people from Scotland: *Scot, Scots, Scotsman, Scottish* |
| | Angus MacPherson is a **Scot** (or **Scotsman**). |
| **STATUE OF LIMITATIONS** | <u>INCORRECT</u>. The correct phrase is *statute of limitations.* |

A 6666*statute of limitations* prescribes the time period in which legal action can take place.

| SUPPOSE TO | Particularly in speech, ***suppose to*** is incorrectly used for ***supposed to***. (INCORRECT: I know I'm ***suppose to*** *exercise.")* |
|---|---|
| | ***Supposed to*** means that something should be done, but often it isn't. ***Suppose*** *(used without* **to***)* means "imagine or expect." |
| | I know I'm **supposed to** exercise, and I **suppose** I'll be sorry if I don't. |

# Tricky
# Singulars
# & Plurals

*"I don't like large groups. I can never remember what our plural is."*

# Using Tricky Singulars & Plurals with Assurance

Often making a word plural is as simple as adding an -s or -es, but when you're dealing with plurals of foreign words, compound nouns, proper names, and numbers and letters, it can get tricky. This chapter will give you the know-how you need to avoid errors.

## Foreign Plurals

English words derived from other languages often have irregular plural forms, although the trend is to Anglicize such words and use the regular –s plural ending. Many scientific terms are derived from Latin or Greek and retain their original endings when used by professionals in the sciences, even though they may be Anglicized in common usage.

Nouns that were "borrowed" from a foreign language often retain their foreign spellings for their plurals. Others have been Anglicized and form plurals by adding –s or -es. Still others have two plurals—an Anglicized plural as well as the original foreign plural. When in doubt about whether or not it is acceptable to use the Anglicized rather the foreign plural, check a dictionary to see which spelling is preferable. In *Merriam Webster's Collegiate Dictionary* (the standard spelling reference for many style guides), the first spelling listed is the preferred spelling for nouns that have two plurals.

Here are some general guidelines on **how to form foreign plurals:**

| | |
|---|---|
| *a →ae* | If the noun ends in *a*, change *a* to *ae*: *alumna/alumnae.* |
| *us→ i* | If the noun ends in *us*, change *us* to *i*: *alumnus/alumni.* |
| *is→es* | If the noun ends in *is*, change *is* to *es*: *crisis/crises.* |
| *on→a* | If the noun ends in *on*, change *on* to *a*: *phenomenon/phenomena.* |
| *um→a* | If the noun ends in *um*, change *um* to *a*: *bacterium/bacteria.* |
| *ix/ex →es* | If the noun ends in *ix* or *ex*, change *ix* or *ex* to *es*: index/indices. (The Anglicized version of nouns ending in *ix* or *ex* adds *es* to the singular form. Anglicized versions usually are acceptable.) |
| *o→i* | If the word ends in *o*, change the *o* to *i*: *libretto/libretti; tempo/tempi; virtuoso/virtuosi; graffito/graffiti.* (Anglicized plurals add *s*: *librettos, librettos, tempos, virtuosos.*) |
| *eau→eaux* | If the word ends in eau, change the eau to eaux. The x is pronounced z: *château/châteaux; gâteau/gâteaux; plateau/plateaux; trousseau/trousseaux* (Anglicized plurals add *-s*: *plateaus, trousseaus.*) |

See the following table for examples of singular and plural forms of nouns derived from foreign languages. When two plurals are listed the preferred plural according to *Webster's* is listed first.

## Singulars & Plurals for Words of Foreign Derivation

| SINGULAR | PLURAL |
| --- | --- |
| addendum | addenda |
| adieu | adieus or adieux |
| alga | algae |
| alumna *(female)* | alumnae *(female)* |
| alumnus *(male)* | alumni *(male)* |
| analysis | analyses |
| antenna | antennae *or* antennas |
| appendix | appendices *or* appendixes |
| automaton | automatons |
| axis | axes |
| bacterium | bacteria |
| basis | bases |
| beau | beaux *or* beaus |
| bureau | bureaus or bureau |

| | |
|---|---|
| cactus | cacti *or* cactuses |
| château | châteaus or châteaux |
| cherub | cherubim *or* cherubs |
| concerto | concerti *or* concertos |
| corpus | corpora |
| cortex | cortices *or* cortexes |
| crisis | crises |
| criterion | criteria |
| curriculum | curricula *or* curriculums |
| datum | data |
| diagnosis | diagnoses |
| dogma | dogmas *or* dogmata |
| ellipsis | ellipses |
| emphasis | emphases |
| encyclopedia | encyclopedias |
| erratum | errata |
| focus | focuses *or* foci |
| formula | formulae *or* formulas |
| forum | forums *or* forma |
| fungus | fungi *or* funguses |
| gâteau | gâteaux |

| | |
|---|---|
| **genus** | genera |
| **hippopotamus** | hippopotamuses *or* hippopotami |
| **honorarium** | honoraria *or* honorariums |
| **hypothesis** | hypotheses |
| **index** | indices *or* indexes |
| **kibbutz** | kibbutzim |
| **larva** | larvae |
| **locus** | loci |
| **matrix** | matrices *or* matrixes |
| **matzo** | matzoth *or* matzos |
| **maximum** | maxima or maximums |
| **medium** *or* ***media*** (***Media*** is now often treated as a singular mass noun.) | media |
| **memorandum** | memorandums *or* memoranda |
| **millennium** | millenniums *or* millennia |
| **minimum** | minima or minimums |
| **minutia** | minutiae |
| **mitzvah** | mitzvoth *or* mitzvahs |

| | |
|---|---|
| **nucleus** | nuclei *or* nucleuses |
| **octopus** | octopuses |
| **parenthesis** | parentheses |
| **persona** | personae *or* personas |
| **phenomenon** | phenomena |
| **plateau** | plateaus or plateaux |
| **platypus** | platypuses |
| **radius** | radii *or* radiuses |
| **referendum** | referenda, referendums |
| **schema** | schemata |
| **seraph** | seraphim *or* seraphs |
| **stadium** | stadia stadiums |
| **stigma** | stigmata *or* stigmas |
| **stimulus** | stimuli |
| **stoma** | stomata *or* stomas |
| **stratum** | strata |
| **syllabus** | syllabuses *or* syllabi |
| **symposium** | symposia *or* symposiums |
| **synopsis** | synopses |
| **synthesis** | syntheses |

| | |
|---|---|
| **tableau** | tableaux |
| **tableau** | tableaux or tableaus |
| **testis** | testes |
| **thesis** | theses |
| **trousseau** | trousseaux *or* trousseaus |
| **ultimatum** | ultimatums *or* ultimata |
| **vertebra** | vertebrae *or* vertebras |
| **vertex** | vertexes *or* vertices |
| **virus** | viruses |
| **vortex** | vortices *or* vortexes |

## Plurals of Compound Nouns

Plurals of compound nouns can be tricky. Which of the words in the compound is made plural? Or, are both words made plural? Such are the pesky questions about plural compounds that annoy writers. Guidelines for forming plural compounds are given below. Some tricky plurals are listed in Webster's, such as fathers-in-law, brothers-in-law, coups d'état, chefs d'oeuvre, and courts-martial.

**1. Compounds written as one word.** Make the final word of the compound plural, usually by adding s or es :

armful/armfuls, birthday/birthdays,
bookshelf/bookshelves, cupful/cupfuls,

222

eyelash/eyelashes, flashback/flashbacks, foothold/footholds, forefoot/forefeet, grandchild/grandchildren, handful/handfuls, hatbox/hatboxes, mousetrap/mousetraps, photocopy/photocopies, printout/printouts, strawberry/strawberries, teaspoonful/teaspoonfuls, toothbrush/toothbrushes, wineglass/wineglasses

**2. Compounds formed by a noun and one or more modifiers.** Make the noun plural. The noun is the chief element in the compound.

deputy chief of staff/deputy chiefs of staff,
deputy sheriff/deputy sheriffs,
editor-in-chief/editors-in-chief,
history account payable/history accounts payable,
adjutant general/adjutants general,
aide-de-camp/aides-de-camp,
assistant attorney/assistant attorneys,
assistant attorney general/assistant attorneys general,
assistant corporation counsel/assistant corporation
  counsels,
  attorney general/attorneys general,
bill of lading/bills of lading,
child wife/child wives,
coup d'état/ coups d'état,
court martial/courts martial,
daughter-in-law/daughters-in-law,
history major/history majors,
leave of absence/leaves of absence,
letter of credit/letters of credit,
lieutenant colonel/lieutenant colonels
looker-on/lookers-on,
major general/major generals,
man-of-war/men-of-war,

passer-by/passers-by,
postmaster general/postmasters general,
president-elect/presidents-elect,
runner-up/runners-up,
secretary general/secretaries general,
senator-elect/senators-elect,
sergeant major/sergeants major,
surgeon general/surgeons general.

## Plurals of Proper Names, Numbers, & Letters

**Names.** Most names are made plural by adding
-s or -es. (Don't use an apostrophe-s to make a
name plural.)

| | | |
|---|---|---|
| the Browns | the Bachs | the IBMs |
| the Intels | the Whites | the Carsons |
| the Mugfords | the Ricardos | the Nickells |

If the name ends in *ch, s, z, x,* or *sh,* add -es to
form the plural. (But omit the -es if it would make
the plural awkward to pronounce: e.g., *Bridges,* not
*Bridgeses.*)

| | | |
|---|---|---|
| the Marches | the Jameses | the Katzes |
| the Maddoxes | the Nashes | the Welshes |

If the name ends in *y,* add -s to form the plural.

| | | |
|---|---|---|
| the Kennedys | the two Marys | the two Kansas Citys |
| the Raffertys | the McCarthys | |

**Numerals & numbers.** When a numeral is used
as a word, add -s *to form the plural.*

| | | |
|---|---|---|
| the 1920s | size 9s | temperatures in the 90s |

When a number is expressed as a word, add -*s* or -*es* to form the plural.

ones      twenty-fives   fifties   sixes

For capital letters and abbreviations consisting of capital letters add -*s* to form the plural.

IQs      three Rs  M.D.s   Ph.D.s   ABCs

For letters that are not capitalized, form the plural by adding *apostrophe-s*. This is done to prevent misreading. (Some style guides add *apostrophe-s* to capitalized nouns, as well.)

o's  p's and q's  c.o.d.'s  dot your i's

 **Try It!**

Rewrite the sentences below to practice changing singulars to plurals. Change each noun in parentheses to the correct plural form. (Some nouns have alternate plurals. In such cases, either is correct.) See page 281 for answers.

**1.** The entertainment, provided by (*alumnus*) and (*alumna*), consisted of two (*concerto*) for oboe and three short (*tableaux*) in which the performers took on the (*persona*) of (*cherub*) and (*seraph*).

**2.** After multiple (*analysis*) of (*datum*) according to agreed-on (*criterion*), we were able to reject the (*hypothesis*) whose (*basis*) rested on defective (*schema*).

**3.** If you could examine the (*corpus*) of the following life forms, which could contain all three of these structures —1. cerebral (*cortex*); 2. (*testis*); and 3. (*vertebra*): (*alga*), (*bacterium*), (*virus*), (*fungus*), (*hippopotamus*), (*larva*), (*octopus*), and (*platypus*)?

4. After sharing (*gateau*) and (*matzo*) with their former (*beau*), Adele and Jeannine said their (*adieu*) and bravely traversed the river's raging (*vortex*) to return to their respective (*château*) on the (*vertex*) of adjoining mountains, where they contemplated their (*trousseau*), stored in massive mahogany (*bureau*).

5. The (*Burgess*), who delighted in (*minutia*) sought to improve their respective (*IQ*) by finding errors in (*encyclopedia*), recording them in (*memorandum*), and submitting them to publishers' (*editor-in-chief*) as (*erratum*) — or to the (*medium*), if publishers made the mistake of ignoring them.

# Words Commonly Misspelled

# Conquer Common Spelling Demons

Do you have any spelling demons? Scan this list of the 495 words most commonly misspelled. Which are you likely to misspell? Make a note of them and focus on the correct spellings.

## A

| | | |
|---|---|---|
| absence | abundance | acceptable |
| accessible | accidentally | acclaim |
| accommodate | accomplish | accordion |
| accumulate | achievement | acquaintance |
| acquire | acquitted | across |
| address | advertisement | advice |
| advise | affect | alleged |
| amateur | analysis | analyze |
| annual | apartment | apparatus |
| apparent | appearance | arctic |
| argument | ascend | atheist |
| attendance | auxiliary | |

## B

| | | |
|---|---|---|
| balloon | barbecue | bargain |
| beneficial- | benefit | biscuit |
| boundaries | | |

# C

calendar

Caribbean

challenge

characteristic

chose

cloth

collectible

coming

commitment

completely

condescend

conscious

controlled

convenient

counselor

criticize

camouflage

category

changeable

chief

cigarette

clothes

colonel

commission

comparative

concede

conscience

consistent

controversial

correlate

courteous

criticism

candidate

cemetery

changing

choose

climbed

clothing

column

committee

competent

condemn

conscientious

continuous

controversy

correspondence

courtesy

# D

deceive

definitely

descend

desirable

develop

defendant

definition

describe

despair

dictionary

deferred

dependent

description

desperate

difference

229

dilemma · dining · disappearance

disappoint · disastrous · discipline

disease · dispensable · dissatisfied

dominant · drunkenness

# E

easily · ecstasy · effect

efficiency · eighth · either

eligible · eliminate · embarrass

emperor · encouragement · enemy

encouraging · entirely · environment

equipped · equivalent · especially

exaggerate · exceed · excellence

exhaust · existence · existent

expense · experience · explanation

extremely · exuberance

# F

facsimile · fallacious · fallacy

familiar · fascinating · feasible

February · fictitious · fiery

finally · financially · fluorescent

forcibly · foreign · foresee

formerly · forfeit · forty

| fourth | fulfill | fundamentally |
|--------|---------|---------------|

## G

| gauge | generally | genius |
|-------|-----------|--------|
| government | governor | grammar |
| grievous | guarantee | guardian |
| guerrilla | guidance | |

## H

| handkerchief | happily | harass |
|--------------|---------|--------|
| height | heinous | hemorrhage |
| heroes | hesitancy | hindrance |
| hoarse | hoping | humorous |
| hygiene | hypocrisy | hypocrite |

## I

| ideally | idiosyncrasy | ignorance |
|---------|--------------|-----------|
| imaginary | immediately | implement |
| incidentally | incredible | independence |
| independent | indicted | indispensable |
| inevitable | influential | information |
| inoculate | intelligence | interference |
| interrupt | introduce | irrelevant |

irresistible    island

# J-K

jealous          judicial          knowledge

# L

laboratory       laid              later
latter           legitimate        leisure
length           license           lieutenant
lightning        likelihood        likely
loneliness       loose             lose
losing           lovely            luxury

# M

magazine         maintain          maintenance
manageable       maneuver          manufacture
marriage         mathematics       medicine
millennium       millionaire       miniature
minuscule        minutes           miscellaneous
mischievous      missile           misspelled
mortgage         mosquito          mosquitoes
murmur           muscle            mysterious

# N

narrative

naturally

necessary

necessity

neighbor

neutron

ninety

ninth

noticeable

nowadays

nuisance

# O

obedience

obstacle

occasion

occasionally

occurred

occurrence

official

omission

omit

omitted

opinion

opponent

opportunity

oppression

optimism

optimistic

orchestra

ordinarily

origin

outrageous

overrun

# P

pamphlets

parallel

particular

pavilion

peaceable

peculiar

penetrate

perceive

performance

permanent

permissible

permitted

perseverance

persistence

personal

perspiration

physical

physician

piece

pilgrimage

pitiful

planning

pleasant

portray

possess

possession

possibility

possible

potato

potatoes

practically

prairie

precede

precedence

preceding

preference

preferred

prejudice

preparation

prescription

prevalent

primitive

principal

principle

privilege

probably

procedure

proceed

profession

professor

prominent

pronounce

pronunciation

propaganda

psychology

publicly

pursue

# Q

quantity

quarantine

questionnaire

quizzes

# R

realistically

realize

really

recede

receipt

receive

recognize

recommend

reference

234

referring relevant relieving

religious remembrance reminiscence

repetition representative resemblance

reservoir resistance restaurant

rheumatism rhythm rhythmical

ridiculous roommate

# S

sacrilegious sacrifice safety

salary satellite scary

scenery schedule secede

secretary seize sense

sentence separate separation

sergeant several severely

shepherd shining siege

similar simile simply

simultaneous sincerely skiing

sophomore souvenir specifically

specimen sponsor spontaneous

statistics stopped strategy

strength strenuous stubbornness

studying subordinate subtle

succeed success succession

| | | |
|---|---|---|
| sufficient | supersede | suppress |
| surprise | surround | susceptible |
| suspicious | syllable | symmetrical |
| synonymous | | |

# T

| | | |
|---|---|---|
| tangible | technical | technique |
| temperamental | temperature | tendency |
| themselves | theories | therefore |
| thorough | though | through |
| tomorrow | tournament | towards |
| tragedy | transferring | tries |
| truly | twelfth | tyranny |

# U

| | | |
|---|---|---|
| unanimous | undoubtedly | unforgettable |
| unique | unnecessary | until |
| usable | usually | utilization |

# V

| | | |
|---|---|---|
| vacuum | valuable | vengeance |
| vigilant | village | villain |

violence          virtue          vision

volume

# W

warrant          warrior          weather

Wednesday        weird            wherever

whether          which            wholly

withdrawal       woman            women

worthwhile       writing

# Y

yacht            yield            young

*Words are chameleons, which reflect the color of their environment.*

*— Learned Hand*

# Answers

## ACCEPT, EXCEPT

1. It's logical to **expect** that an Oscar-caliber actor would not **accept** a role in a ridiculously bad movie **except** under dire circumstances.
2. Thus, **except** for die-hard John Wayne fans, few movie-goers could **accept** Wayne in the incongruous role of Genghis Khan in *The Conqueror*.
3. Critics did not **except** director Dick Powell from responsibility for the absurd Asian Western.
4. Evidently Powell was willing to **accept** Wayne's statement that he saw *The Conqueror* as a cowboy film and would play Khan as a gunslinger, **except** that he slung a sword.
5. **Except** for transporting the Gobi Desert to Utah, **except** for the preposterous casting of the Duke as Genghis Khan and Susan Hayward as a Tartar princess, viewers might have been willing to **accept** the premise of the film.

## ACUTE, CHRONIC

1. Could the **chronic** fatigue I have been plagued with for years be caused by an allergy?
2. The dog's **acute** sense of smell quickly picked up the suspect's trail through the woods.
3. Your **chronic** lateness will get you fired!
4. She was immediately sent to the hospital for an **acute** attack of appendicitis.

5. Gifted with **acute** intelligence, the chimp easily won the game of checkers from his partner, whose **chronic** hyperactivity interfered with her concentration.
6. A broken arm is an example of a medical condition that is **acute**. Recurring asthma is **chronic**.

## ADVICE, ADVISE

1. Do you need an expert to **advise** you on how to solve your problem?
2. Much **advice** is available on what to do when your dog has a skunk encounter.
3. The **advice** given by most dog owners is to saturate your pet in tomato juice; others **advise** using vinegar.
4. Both pieces of **advice** simply distract the nose without curing the problem.
5. What do veterinarians **advise**?
6. Their **advice** is to mix the following in an open container: 1 quart of 3% hydrogen peroxide, ¼ cup baking soda, and 1-2 tsps. of mild dishwashing detergent that does not contain ammonia or bleach.
7. They **advise** saturating your pet's coat with the mixture, then let it set 5 minutes before rinsing.
8. One last piece of **advice** is to not keep the mixture in a closed container because it can explode.

## AFFECT, EFFECT

1. We are all familiar with the **effect** of biting into a red-hot chili pepper.
2. We may **affect** indifference, but our taste buds **effect** a protest to the fiery-hot **effect** of capsaicin, the ingredient that causes red-hots to **affect** us with their built-in fire.
3. But that fiery **effect** may **affect** us in beneficial ways.
4. New studies point to capsaicin's detrimental **effect** on cancer cells.
5. For malignant cells, capsaicin can **effect** a premature "death."

6. Capsaicin's fiery **effect** is put to use in a barnacle repellant applied to boats.
7. Capsaicin can **affect** and dull the perception of pain, an anesthetic **effect**.

## AGGRAVATE, IRRITATE
1. Did Jean's remarks **irritate** John?
2. Did John's temper tantrum **aggravate** a bad situation?*
3. Poison ivy can **irritate** the skin.
4. Can unusual stress **aggravate** acne?
5. Neglect of agriculture can **aggravate** poverty.
6. Little things do not seem to **irritate** him.
7. Be careful not to **aggravate** your back pain by lifting those heavy boxes.
8. Is he simply in a bad mood, or have I done something to **irritate** him?

## ALIBI, EXCUSE
1. He found himself trying to find an **excuse** to believe the lie she had told him.
2. Do you have an **alibi** for the time of the crime?
3. In case he got caught, Higgins tried to think of a believable **excuse** for why he stashed a change of clothes and false mustache in his car trunk.
4. What **alibi** did Higgins concoct to convince others he was elsewhere at the time of the crime?
5. Higgins is the only suspect whose **alibi** of where he was that night was proved false.
6. What was his **excuse** for giving false information to the F.B.I about his whereabouts?
7. The F.B.I. immediately dismissed Higgins's **excuse** that he gave them a false **alibi** because he was too embarrassed to admit the truth.
8. Although not having an **alibi** for the time of a crime is not illegal, it isn't nice to lie to the F.B.I.

## ALL READY, ALREADY

1. Are you **all ready** for the big one—an event bigger than the predicted big earthquake in California?
2. This is something that **already** occurred before, some 65 million years ago, when the Earth was **already** into the Age of Dinosaurs.
3. An asteroid collided with Earth, producing a dust cloud and resulting cold temperatures that killed thousands of species—and, we are **already** overdue for another such collision.
4. Preparations have **already** started to ensure we will be **all ready** to prevent our extinction when the next one arrives.
5. We **already** scan the skies for asteroids.
6. We are making plans so that we will be **all ready** to divert asteroids with missiles.
7. Preparations are **already** being made to avoid a collision so that we will be **all ready** for it.


## ALL TOGETHER, ALTOGETHER

1. Are you **altogether** positive that Henry is missing?
2. We did not stay **all together** as a group all the time.
3. I am **altogether** certain Henry was with us when we left.
4. I distinctly remember us being **all together** on the dock.
5. I think we were **all together** when we boarded the ship, but I am not **altogether** positive.
6. We were not **all together** at the lifeboat drill, and I am sure I did not see Henry there.
7. We went to his room **all together** but found it empty.
8 Henry is **altogether** besotted with Alexandra, but had he stayed behind to be with her or been abducted?

## A LOT, ALLOT

1. If you **allot** time for regular exercise, you will no doubt feel **a lot** better.
2. Work becomes **a lot** easier when you **allot** some of it to others.
3. **A lot** of people manage to talk **a lot** without saying much of anything.
4. If you **allot** an acre for corn, you will still have **a lot** of acreage for other crops.

## AMONG, BETWEEN

1. The nearest pharmacy is **between** the grocery store and the pet store.
2. We divided the reward money **among** the three of us.
3. Warning! **Among** the beautiful flowers in our gardens are four that can be deadly.
4. Is that foxglove **between** the two rosebushes?
5. Careful—its flowers are **among** the most poisonous if you eat them.
6. The charming autumn crocus is **among** the few flowers that bloom before they have leaves.
7. But autumn crocus flowers are poisonous and have caused several deaths **among** those who found them in the woods and tried to eat them.
8. The beautiful flowers of oleander and angel's trumpet are **among** the garden's most deadly.
9. **Among** the beauties of the garden lie some hazards, but only if you eat the flowers.

## ASSURE, ENSURE, INSURE

1. Do you need to **insure** the contents of this package?
2. Send your letter by Priority Mail to **ensure** that it arrives by Friday.
3. Let me **assure** you that I will **insure** the vase against loss, and I will double-box it to **ensure** its safe delivery.
4. Be sure to **assure** students that our correspondence course will help **ensure** their success in picking the right stocks.
5. Did you **insure** your house for its replacement value?


## A WHILE, AWHILE

1. The plan is to continue working **awhile** and then break for lunch.
2. Once in **a while** I think of Cape Cod and begrudge the fact that it has been **a while** since I've been able to take a vacation.
3. I would love to sit **awhile** and watch the sun set on Cape Cod Bay.
4. Since it may take **a while** to catch a fish, let's plan on being here for **a while**.
5. We'll fish **awhile**, and in **a while** we'll head for shore.
6. Will you think of me once in **a while**?
7. Children, please sit down and be quiet for **a while**


## BAD, BADLY

1. The musicians performed **badly** at rehearsal.
2. She felt **bad** about her mistake.
3. He was **badly** scarred after a **bad** encounter with a grizzly bear.
4. Mandrake was an evil tyrant, **bad** from birth, who treated his subjects **badly.**
5. I was **badly** distressed on learning that he had paid me with a **bad** egan pelting the stage with rotten bananas and **bad** tomatoes.

## BRAKE(S), BREAK(S)

1. When you want to wish an actor good luck you say, "**Break a leg!**"
2. Don't step on the **brake** pedal when you're on a patch of ice.
3. The team got the **break** they needed to **break** their losing streak.
4. The car's **brake** fluid leaked out because of a **break** in its **brake** hose, and the **brakes** wouldn't work.
5. In a truck or train, pressurized air, not fluid, is used to put on the **brakes**.
6. Josh has never been known to **break** a rule.

## BRING, TAKE

1. **Take** this to the bank and **bring** back a receipt.
2. In the 1920s, Charles Ponzi promised to **bring** investors a 100% return in 30 days.
3. Thousands of greedy, gullible investors were only too happy to **bring** their money to Ponzi.
4. They thought he would **take** it to invest.
5. In reality, he used it to pay former investors, who expected him to **bring** them a "return."
6. It was inevitable that the scheme would one day collapse and **bring** the authorities to Ponzi's door.
7. Ponzi's schemes were destined to first **take** him away to court, and from there, **take** him to the hoosegow.
8. Ponzi's stint in the cooler did not **bring** Ponzi lasting disgrace, for he later landed a job with Alitalia Airlines.

## CAN, MAY

1. You **may** come into my garden to look at the flowers, but beware!

2. The beautiful foxglove flowers are poisonous. They **can** kill you
3. You **may** look, touch, and smell. But don't eat them unless you **can** withstand the stress and discomfort of a wildly racing heart.
4. On the other hand, foxglove is the source of digitalis, which **can** strengthen the heart.

## CAPITAL, CAPITOL
1. What is the **capital** of New Jersey?
2. The state **capitol** is made of granite.
3. Proposed changes to the **capital** gains tax are under discussion on **Capitol** Hill in the nation's **capital**.
4. Should the name of a pet begin with a **capital** letter?

## CENSOR, CENSURE
1. The TV **censor** deleted a segment from the sitcom.
2. During the war, a **censor** checked soldiers' outgoing letters for information of benefit to the enemy.
3. It is unusual for such a prominent politician to escape criticism and **censure**.
4. According to Demosthenes, the most effective way to get rid of **censure** is to correct ourselves.
5. What do you think Juvenal meant when he said that **censure** acquits the raven, but pursues the dove?

6. Please **censor** your outrageous, offensive remarks in front of the children!

7. According to one newscaster, twenty-two percent of the people in the United States believe that the government should **censor** newspapers.
8. Do you agree with Gilmore Simms that the dread of **censure** is the death of genius?
9. The rude remark had left my lips before I was able to **censor** it.
10. He felt an uncontrollable need to **censure** others, to express his extreme disapproval.
11. You need to **censor** some of your content if you are intending to publish your book for children.
12. As soon as the letter had been sent, I wanted to **censor** it, to call it back, to change my wording.
13. The only thing that holds his bad behavior in check is his fear of **censure**.
14. The **censor** struck out two scenes from the film.

## CHORD, CORD

1. Do you have a **cord** long enough go around a **cord** of wood, which is 4 by 4 by 8 feet?
2. The sonata's opening **chord** progression set a plaintive note that struck a responsive **chord** in the audience.
3. Fortunately, his spinal **cord** was not injured when a **cord** of wood fell off the truck on top of him.
4. His unfortunate demonstration of the fire hazards of overloading an electrical outlet struck a **chord** of alarm in the audience.
5. The demonstration—which consisted of plugging in a power **cord** from a space heater plus an extension **cord** to which was attached the electric **cord** to a toaster and the **cord** to a hair-dryer—proved the old adage about where there's smoke, there's fire!

## CITE, SIGHT, SITE

1. We're standing on the **site** of the first schoolhouse in Tennessee.
2. What a **sight** to be on the **site** at Cape Canaveral when a space shuttle is launched!
3. To **cite** the sentiments of George Bernard Shaw, "Beauty is all very well at first **sight**; but who ever looks at it when it has been in the house for three days?"
4. Can you **cite** an example of a Web **site** that gives information on the senses of hearing and **sight** of the various reptiles?
5. Go to NASCAR.com, the official **site** of NASCAR, to see dramatic shots of the Bristol Motor Speedway, an amazing **sight** for the eyes, which many **cite** as the "Coliseum of Confusion."
6. To **cite** the words of racing legend Mario Andretti, "Circumstances may cause interruptions and delays, but never lose **sight** of your goal."
7. Can you **cite** a few examples in support of your argument?
8. We need to be cautious and stay out of **sight**.

**COARSE, COURSE**
1. Does the **course** of true love ever run smooth?
2. The film's **coarse** language was edited for TV.
3. You'll find Harry on the golf **course**, of **course**.
4. The **course** is required in order to get your degree.
. Our ship's **course** is set, and we'll arrive in due **course**.

## COMPARE, CONTRAST

1. Adjust the TV picture so there is less **contrast**.
2. In **contrast** to her blonde twin sister, Kim has red hair.
3. If you **compare** the two photographs of the oak tree, you'll see that the one on the right has more **contrast**.
4. Obviously, Jack and Jill are not identical twins, but if you **compare** them, you'll find that their facial features are similar.

5. If an essay question asks you to **contrast** the pre-Civil War economies of the North versus the South, it is asking you to discuss their differences.
6. If you **compare** an armadillo to a turtle, you will see that each has a kind of protective armor, or "shell."
7. But whereas the armadillo is warm-blooded and a mammal, the turtle, in **contrast**, is cold-blooded and a reptile.

## COMPLEMENT, COMPLIMENT

Early in the game, cereal manufacturers learned to use the cereal box to distinguish a product from its competitors and to **complement** its contents. Both celebrities and cartoon characters were paid the **compliment** of being a product's mascot. Mascots were chosen to **complement** the product's perceived features. For example, the choice of Norman Rockwell to paint a red-haired, freckle-faced boy for Kellogg's Corn Flakes, was a **compliment** to Rockwell's ability to project a homey, family image that would **complement** the message, "Buy Kellogg's Corn Flakes for your kids." Even the box's background color, white, was chosen to **complement** the pure, clean image targeted for the product, just as yellow was chosen as a **complement** for the cheerful, energy-packed image designed for Kellogg's Sugar Corn Pops. For many reasons, high sales of a boxed cereal are a **compliment** to its designer's ability to effectively **complement** the product's personality, or image.

## COMPOSE, COMPRISE

1. Orchestras **comprise** four groups of instruments: strings, woodwinds, brass, and percussion.
2. She began to **compose** a "Dear John" letter to Harry.
3. These books **comprise** all that remains of his library.
4. Eleven of the finest players **compose** the All-Star Team.

5. What four bodies of water **compose** the Great Lakes?

**CONNOTE, DENOTE**
1. What kind of animal does the word *dog* **denote**?
2. The word *mutt* is a synonym for *dog*, but what negative or positive associations does the word *mutt* **connote**?
3. Both *skinny* and *svelte* **denote** thinness, but they do not **connote** the same view of that quality.
4. Would you choose the word *thrifty* or *miserly* to **connote** a positive view of someone who is careful about spending money?
5. A copywriter carefully chooses words that **connote** positive associations.
6. That symbol on the sign is used to **connote** danger.
7. The perfume's name is meant to **connote** luxury.

**CONTINUAL, CONTINUOUS**
1. The **continuous** barking of that dog is an annoyance.
2. There is a **continuous** stream of traffic downtown.
3. She listened to the **continual** rush of water over the dam, punctuated by a **continuous** stop-and-start buzz of a saw.
4. The uninterrupted, **continual** loud music from the apartment was a source of constant irritation.
5. The speaker droned on interminably in a **continual** monotone in spite of **continuous** attempts to cut him off.

**COUNCIL, COUNSEL**
1. When O'Reilly was in high school, he was elected to the student **council**.
2. Let's hold a **counsel** to decide how to present our plan to city **council**.
3. I am seeking your **counsel** on how to find a **counsel** for the defense.
4. Her **counsel** was that it was advisable to seek the **counsel** of an attorney who has expertise in such matters.

5. On advice of **counsel**, the **council** decided not to allocate any more funds for the questionable project.
6. Her **counsel** advised her that she should first seek **counsel** from an expert and then approach the town **council**.

## DESERT, DESSERT
1. Please don't **desert** me on this dry, arid **desert**.
2. They say that rats **desert** a sinking ship.
3. Harvey received his just **deserts** tonight for his naughty behavior: no **dessert** after supper and no TV or electronic games.
4. If you violate your orders and **desert** your military post, albeit in a sweltering, uninhabitable **desert**, the army will see that you get your just **deserts**, which will be sweet, like a **dessert** sweet.
5. He said he would never **desert** her, as they stood on their **desert** island, looking over the ocean for ships.

## DEVICE, DEVISE

1. He tried to **devise** a foolproof plan to pick the winning lottery number.
2. This state-of-the-art optical **device** will enable you to read a newspaper from across a football field.
3. Can you **devise** a **device** to open a padlock that has a combination lock?
4. During the Cold War, the proliferation of spies engendered a need to **devise** tools for spies.
5. The need to **devise** a **device** to conceal a weapon produced the fake cigarette pack, a **device** that concealed a one-shot 22 caliber pistol.
6. Since a spy may need to **devise** an escape plan, the CIA was able to successfully **devise** a unique means of escape. More than a simple **device**, it was an inflatable single-engine plane that inflated in under 6 minutes and could fly up to 70 mph.

## DISINTERE-STED, UNINTERESTED

1. We need impartial, **disinterested** fact-finders to help resolve this controversy.
2. I find it difficult to make myself study if I am **uninterested** in the subject.
3. Don't ask me about the mayoral race, since I am absolutely **uninterested** in politics.
4. Far from being **uninterested**, Milbridge eats up local politics, although you might expect him to be a **disinterested** spectator, since he hails from the British Isles.
5. Since I am **uninterested** in anything to do with math, I am **uninterested** in taking a course in statistics.
6. To render a fair decision, a judge must be **disinterested** and impartial.
7. The ruler found it hard to get **disinterested** advice from any of his counselors.
8. He was **uninterested** in our discussion about local politics, but we tried to get his opinion as a **disinterested** citizen of another state.

## E.G., I.E.

1. The fourth president of the United States, **i.e.**, James Madison, served for two terms.
2. Some insects can sting, **e.g.**, ants, bees, wasps, and hornets.
3. Tourist attractions, **e.g.**, beaches, resort casinos, Revolutionary War sites, and the Pine Barrens, abound in the Garden State, **i.e.**, New Jersey.
4. Ascorbic acid, **i.e.**, Vitamin C, helps heal wounds and aids in maintaining health, **e.g.**, by resisting infection from certain viruses and bacteria.
5. There is a vaccine available for pertussis, **i.e.**, whooping cough, which is a highly contagious disease spread through

the air, **e.g.**, by coughing, sneezing, or breathing in someone's face.

## ELICIT, ILLICIT
1. **Illicit** copies of the CD will **elicit** outrage if we sell it.
2. His quote is sure to **elicit** outrage if we print it.
3. We must **elicit** public support to stop **illicit** sales of cigarettes to minors.
4. When his **illicit** investment scheme is exposed, it is sure to **elicit** angry responses from irate investors.
5. Once the senator's **illicit** tax-evasion scheme is exposed, it is doubtful that she will still **elicit** the support of her constituents.
6. The sales letter did not **elicit** any responses yet.
7. The arrest was for possession of **illicit** drugs.
8. The phone calls were intended to **elicit** information on how people were going to vote.
9. This photo of the sad-eyed puppy is guaranteed to **elicit** sympathy.
10. The police confiscated over $200,000 in **illicit** profits made in his **illicit** business activities.
11. What information does the survey intend to **elicit** from the respondents?

## EMIGRATE, IMMIGRATE
1. If you **emigrate** from the United States and **immigrate** to Canada, will you lose your U.S. citizenship?
2. In 1849, the California Gold Rush prompted poverty-stricken laborers to **emigrate** from China and **immigrate** to the United States.
3. By the 1870s, gold had become scarce, the economy was in a steep decline, and laborers who been lured to **immigrate** to California became scapegoats.
4. In particular, animosity was directed toward those who had been lured to **emigrate** from China.

5. This resulted in the Chinese Exclusion Act, which barred those who tried to **emigrate** from China and **immigrate** to the United States.
6. In 1795 they decided to **emigrate** from their homeland and **immigrate** to America.

## EMPATHY, SYMPATHY

1. They were deeply moved by **sympathy** for the sufferings of the flood victims.
2. It is hard to feel **sympathy** for someone whose misfortune was caused by his own reckless behavior.
3. I feel **empathy** for those who have a fear of public speaking even though I don't suffer from that particular phobia.
4. The teacher has **empathy** for students who have reading comprehension difficulties.
5. He struggled to find words to express his heartfelt **sympathy.**
6. He expressed **sympathy** for the earthquake victims.
7. Please accept our **sympathy** for your loss.

## EVERY DAY, EVERYDAY

1. George follows the same routine **every day** when he wakes up.
2. Since the dance is not formal, you may wear your **everyday** clothes.
3. If you use this product faithfully **every day**, you will be amazed at the results.
4. Undoubtedly you have discovered that **everyday** remedies don't work.
5. You can apply lemon juice to your freckles **every day**, and the only benefit will be to the lemon growers.
6. We receive glowing reports from users of Freckles Be Gone **every day**.
7. Since the sun shines **every day**, slap on some Freckles Be Gone as an **everyday** precaution before venturing outside.

8. Make Freckles Be Gone part of your **everyday** skin care program, and your skin will thank you **every day**.

## EVERY ONE, EVERYONE

1. A fad is something that sweeps **everyone** away for a brief time before it fades away and **every one** of its devotees forgets about it.
2. In 1958, when Wham-O, Inc. introduced its Hula Hoop® to America, **every one** of the first twenty million was sold in six months for $1.98 each.
3. During the 1960s, with the Hula Hoop® craze in full swing; **everyone** who had hips and the inclination was hula hooping.
4. Not **everyone** who tried to hula hoop succeeded.
5. The hip rotating craze was not admired by **everyone**, as evidenced by Japan's banning it on the grounds of indecency.
6. On March 3, 1939, Harvard freshman Lothrop Withington, Jr., swallowed a live goldfish on a $10 bet, starting a craze that **everyone** condemned.
7. Goldfish swallowing soon swamped college campuses and was indulged in by **everyone** game enough to try it.
8. Image the outrage of **everyone** (or **every one**) who had ever owned or admired a goldfish!

## FARTHER, FURTHER

1. In the 1920s, astronaut Edwin Hubbell discovered that galaxies around us were moving **farther** from the Earth.
2. **Further**, by observing patterns of color in the sky and how those colors shifted in the nearer and **farther** galaxies, he was led to the conclusion that the universe was expanding uniformly. In 1998, using larger telescopes, astronomers made a **further** discovery. The **farther** galaxies were moving **farther** away from Earth much faster than

expected. Yes, the universe was expanding, but **further**, the expansion was accelerating.

3. The **farther** ahead we look in time, the **farther** the distance between galaxies.
4. If we could look **farther** into the future, we might see it happening in approximately a trillion times a fifty-year lifespan.

### FEWER, LESS

1. In 1793 the French adopted a metric 10-hour day, so that a day had 14 hours **fewer** than before.
2. Although each day had **fewer** hours, each hour had no **less** time because an hour was 100 minutes. In addition, every month had three weeks, which was **fewer** weeks than before.
3. Each week had 10 days, so that every month had 30 days. No month had **fewer**.
4. A logical system, *n'est-ce pas*? Seemingly, it would cause **less** confusion and **fewer** missed appointments.
5. The system, a triumph of French logic, was not to last but was abandoned by no **less** a personage than Napoleon Bonaparte, shortly after he was crowned emperor in 1804.

### FOREWORD, FORWARD

1. The preface of a book is written by the author, but the book's **foreword** is written by someone else.
2. We cannot move **forward** until we agree on a plan.
3. After reading the book's intriguing **foreword**, I looked **forward** to reading what the author had to say,
4. I wanted to find out for myself whether the book's **foreword** had exaggerated the book's appeal to **forward**-thinking readers, who envision moving **forward** to the day when humans colonize Mars.

5. Always put your best foot **forward**.
6. I will be honored to write the **foreword**.
7. He leaned **forward** to hear what she was saying.
8. A famous American historian wrote the **foreword** to the second edition.


## FORMALLY, FORMERLY

1. He was **formerly** known as "Sweeney" before **formally** changing his name.
2. Although I never replied **formally** to his written invitation, I **formerly** mentioned to him that I would attend his graduation.
3. Winthorpe, **formerly** casual and careless about his appearance, was transformed after meeting the **formally** elegant Caroline
4. His **formerly** disreputable trench coat was gone, and in its place, a **formally** cut Savile Row topcoat, the apotheosis of elegance and style.


## FORTUITOUS, FORTUNATE

1. The **fortuitous** circumstance of having a doctor in the house was truly **fortunate**.
2. How **fortuitous** to find that money just when I needed it!
3. She is indeed **fortunate** to have a supportive family.
4. Taking that advanced biology course turned out to be **fortuitous**.
5. This new bill is designed to help for the less **fortunate**.
6. It was **fortunate** we left before the blizzard arrived.

## GOOD, WELL

Typically, during severe droughts, lightning ignites wildfires that ravage the Okefenokee Swamp. Since **good** methods of fire retardation work **well** to combat wildfires, it would be a **good** idea to use them. Right? Not necessarily. Natural fires are **good** for the Okefenokee and are necessary to keep the swamp "healthy" and **well**. In fact, without wildfires, the Okefenokee would cease to exist. Fires clear the swamp of shrubs, small trees, and layers of peat several feet deep, whose gradual buildup would otherwise choke the swamp. The burning of peat has a **good** result. It reveals open lakes. The destruction of small trees is **good** for the growth of the classic tree of the Okefenokee, the large cypress (which is fire resistant.) As far as wildfires in the Okefenokee are concerned, perhaps it's fair to say that all's **well** that ends **well**.

## HANGED, HUNG

1. We washed the muddy clothes and **hung** them out to dry.
2. The outlaw was sentenced to be **hanged**.
3. When hanging pictures, use a level to make sure they are **hung** straight.
4. The famous "hanging judge," Arkansas's Isaac Parker, ordered 160 executions, of which 79 were carried out and the 79 sentenced were **hanged**.
5. The keys were **hung** on hooks attached to the closet door.
6. During the days of the "Old West," many of the outlaws were **hanged**.
7. The man convinced of poisoning the king was **hanged**.
8. I almost **hung** up the phone, but the urgency in her voice made me decide to hang on.
9. They were **hanged** when their assassination plot was discovered.

## HEALTHFUL, HEALTHY

1. Which is more **healthful**, cheesecake or fried green tomatoes?
2. If you want to be **healthy**, exercise regularly.

258

-3. Eat a **healthful** diet in order to achieve optimum health and stay healthy.
4. Here the **healthful** climate attracts those who want to feel **healthy** again.
5. These **healthful** foods should be included in your diet on your road to health.
6. You need to cut down on sugar and eat **healthful** foods if you want to be **healthy**.
7. Eat a **healthful** diet, exercise regularly, and get a good night's sleep to stay **healthy**.


## HISTORIC, HISTORICAL

1. The letter is not a **historic** document. Its **historical** interest lies in the fact that it was written by Martha Washington.
2. The famous phrase "the shot heard 'round the world" is a **historic** reference to the opening shot of the Revolutionary War.
3. That **historic** shot was fired on April 19, 1775, in Lexington, Massachusetts when the British encountered American militiamen who refused to disperse.
4. Although there is no **historical** evidence as to who fired that **historic** shot, it was followed by others, and eight Americans lay dead.
5. That **historic** event in Lexington marked the beginning of America's fight for independence.

## I, ME
1. Maurice and **I** went back to Boston, where he and **I** first met.
2. Do you believe him or **me**?
3. Between you and **me**, George, Andrea, and **I** are enlisting in the navy.
4. Will you feed the dog for Bernie and **me** if he and **I** decide to go to the fair?
5. Among Dean, Josh, Greg, and **I**, only Dean and **me** ordered dessert.

## IMPLY, INFER
1. What clues lead you to **infer** that Schultz has recently visited India?
2. Does that raised eyebrow **imply** you are a skeptic in regard to astrology?
3. I hope you did not **infer** from my remark that I think you should diet. "Pleasingly plump" was not meant to **imply** anything of the kind.
4. Indeed, we may **infer** from numerous examples in the animal kingdom that the tendency to store fat may **imply** a superior genetic ability to survive famine.
5. You may, however, **infer** that I meant to **imply** that I find you pleasingly attractive.
6. I hope you will **infer** that my awkwardly stated remark was meant as a compliment.

## ITS, IT'S
l. If **it's** Tuesday, this must be Belgium.
2. Can you name this place? **Its** name comes from the Middle English word for "rabbit."
3. **It's** been called "America's Playground," known worldwide for **its** hot dogs, **its** Cyclone Roller Coaster, Mermaid Parade, and Deno's Wonderwheel. **It's** the one and only Coney Island. **Its** reputation was well deserved.

## JEALOUS, ZEALOUS

1. A **zealous** reporter exposed corrupt officials who had taken kickbacks.
2. Wishing to appear **zealous**, Frank made a show of taking work home every night.
3. Would you be **jealous** if I told you I had just won the Power Ball lottery?
4. Catherine was a fervent and **zealous** reformer and was known to be a **zealous** advocate of women's rights.
5. In spite of Alvin's **zealous** attempts to get to the root of her problem, Alvina continued to feel **jealous** and insecure in their relationship.
6. Geraldine had become increasingly **zealous** in her determined attempts to reform Fred.
7. He was a **zealous** defender of his beliefs, in spite of almost overwhelming resistance.


## JUDICIAL, JUDICIOUS

1. Do you believe that all juries are **judicious** in rendering a verdict or in awarding damage awards?
2. Was it **judicious** for an Austin, Texas, jury to award $780,000 to a woman who broke her ankle tripping over her toddler in a furniture store?
3. If lawyers would be more **judicious** in the cases they accept, our **judicial** system would not be swamped with frivolous lawsuits.
4. Lawyers were **judicious** in refusing to accept the $380 million lawsuit against Michael Jordan by a man who claimed Jordan looked like him.
5. A **judicious** use of mouthwash is recommended for garlic lovers in Indiana, where it is illegal to enter a movie theater or public streetcar within four hours of eating garlic.

6. Perhaps the Vermont law requiring citizens to take at least one bath a week—on Saturday night—should be subjected to **judicial** review.

## KEY, QUAY
1. We walked along the wide cement **quay** that paralleled the riverbank.
2. The **key** to relaxation is deep breathing.
3. I think this skeleton **key** will unlock the door at the back of the shed.
4. This small red feather is the **key** to the solution of the mystery.
5. As she was getting off the ship docked at the **quay**, the **key** to her car fell from her hand and into the murky water.
6. Those small islands are the **key** I was referring to, not the **key** to the cabin.
7. You will find beautiful ornamental gardens and sandy beaches on the **quay**.

## LAY, LIE
1. Who **lay** that wet washcloth on my wood table?
2. Yes, I cannot tell a **lie**, but I did not mean to let the wet cloth **lie** there.
3. The husky **lay** down its bone and then **lay** down beside it.
4. I'll **lay** the towel on the sand so I can **lie** on it.
5. Before you **lie** down, **lay** the remote control on top of the TV.
6. She **lay** awake for hours, unable to sleep.
7. What danger **lies** (or **lay**) around the corner?
8. You'd better **lie** down if you feel faint.
9. If you **lay** those scarves on the top shelf, they may **lie** there indefinitely before being sold.
10. If you are really willing to tell the truth, why are you unwilling to take a **lie** detector test?

11. Those piles of trash will **lie** along the street until they are colle--cted.

## LEAD, LED

1. We need someone who will take the **lead** and **lead** us back to the cabin.
2. If we had not been **led** astray by moose tracks, we would be there by now.
3. Who's playing the male **lead** in the drama?
4. **Lead** them to the nearest exit.
5. Which is the path that will **lead** us to the cave?
6. What are the symptoms of **lead** poisoning?
7. If we follow the river, it will **lead** us to the sea.
8. We need to find a new **lead** singer tonight because Rocque has laryngitis.
9. The value of that stock turned out to be less than we were **led** to believe.
10. That one unfortunate mistake **led** to the general's defeat.
11. Who will **lead** the team to victory?
12. Myles was chosen to **lead** the investigation into the mysterious death of Styles. In his capacity as Inspector, he had **led** many investigations in the past. Did the **lead** pipe lying near the body **lead** him to suspect that Styles' death was no accident? Was it the dagger under the sofa? No, neither would have **led** Myles to pronounce that it was death by poisoning. Rather, it was the faint smell of almonds in Styles' overturned glass that was the **lead** Myles needed. It **led** him to suspect cyanide as the agent of death. That faint odor, similar to that of peach pits, **led** to the eventual arrest of the murderer.

## LEAVE, LET

1. Please **let** me help you with that heavy package.
2. If we **leave** now, we'll beat the exit crowds.
3. We'll **leave** the question for now.

4. We need to **leave** early to catch our plane.
5. Are you willing to **leave** what happens to chance?
6. There is an old saying, "**Let** sleeping dogs lie."
7. The hotel won't **let** us check in until 2:00 p.m.
8. We may **leave** our baggage with them, however.
9. I hope I didn't **leave** my toothbrush at home.
10. If only I had **let** the phone ring, I wouldn't have left it behind.
11. I don't suppose you'd **let** me borrow yours?
12. Why did I even ask — except that I must have taken **leave** of my senses!
13. I always **leave** something behind.
14. I'll **leave** it all to you, Mr. Perfect!
15. Now **let** me be. I want to sulk for a while.

**LIKE, AS, AS IF**
1. Who was it who said. "Nothing spoils a party **like** a genius"?
2. You look **as if** you've seen a ghost.
3. Was that remark meant **as** a joke?
4. Don't talk to me **as if** I were a child.
5. It looks **as if** we might be in for some violent weather tomorrow.
6. He's **as** busy **as** he ever was.
7. I can't imagine why he thought he could hide a thing **like** that from you.
8. Greg decided, **like** Allen, to join the club.
9. They thought of themselves **as** star-crossed lovers, **like** Romeo and Juliet.
10. The girl in the photograph does look **like** her.
11. Allison looks **like** her mother.
12. **As** I told you earlier, your test will be on Friday.
13. We need to hire more people **like** you, **as** you might have heard before.

14. **As** they like to say, "There's no business **like** show business!"
15. There's no time **like** the present, is there?
16. They were late again, **as** usual.
17. Joe blocks the linebacker **like** a pro.
18. Is jealousy **like** a green-eyed monster, **as** William Shakespeare said?
19. That looks **like** a diamond, but it might be a fake.
20. **As** I was once told: If it fogs up **like** a foggy mirror when you breathe on it for 2-4 seconds, it is not a diamond, but glass.

## LOOSE, LOSE

1. I hope you didn't **lose** the key to the safe.
2. The dog got **loose** because its collar was too **loose**.
3. In the 1890's the invention of the safety bicycle—comfortable, fast, and with air-filled tires—was the Victorian woman's passport to **loose** the shackles of house and husband and **lose** herself in the joys of two-wheeling it, if only around town. To Victorians, who were so straight-laced that a **loose** woman was one who went without corsets, the bicycle was a threat that would tempt women to **lose** their frailty, femininity, and male-dependency—perhaps even their virtue. Victorian women took to bicycling like wild birds let **loose** from a cage take to flight. Despite heckling, jeers, and even stoning, they did not **lose** their zest for the sport. They did **lose** pounds of underwear and long, interfering skirts. In 1898 the Rational Dress Society approved seven pounds as the maximum weight of a woman's underclothing. Victorian fashion could not help but **lose** to the new "rational" fashion, exemplified by Bloomers (gasp!) and split skirts.

## MAY. MIGHT

1. My homework **might** (or **may**) be in my locker, or a passing raven **might** have flown off with it.
2. He **might** have lived to be a hundred if only he had listened to me.
3. It **may** be that hummingbirds find the color red especially attractive.
4. If the ball game hadn't been rained out, we **might** have won.
5. Since Hurricane Elva **may** arrive on Wednesday, it **may** (or **might**) be a good idea to buy bottled water today.
6. I **may (or might) take** a lunch break if we're not too busy.
7. I **might** always win millions in the lottery — you never know!
8. I **might** have gone to see that film, but I saw its bad reviews first.
9. Before long, humans **might** vacation on Mars!

## NAVAL, NAVEL

1. The **navel** is the center of our physical bodies.
2. In 1776, England was a great **naval** power.
3. This **naval** telescope collapses to fit in a sailor's **navel**.
4. If you are an omphalocentric, you practice contemplating your **navel** as an aid to meditation.
5. The battleship became the symbol of **naval** power and dominance.
6. A jewel adorned the belly-dancer's **navel**.
7. The dockyard covers 50 acres and is used primarily for **naval** repairs.
8. She has received commission as a **naval** officer.
9. The sailors were all transferred to the American **naval** base at Guantanamo.
10. The statue was painted with elaborate designs from **navel** to foot.

11. Some say a large boulder on Easter Island in Chile is the "**navel** of the world."

## NOISOME, NOISY

1. At the ballgame, the **noisy** yells of the fans assaulted my ears, while the **noisome** aromas of sweat and sauerkraut offended my nose.
2. The room was so **noisy** I couldn't hear myself think.
3. The **noisome** aroma of *eau-de-skunk* dampened my enthusiasm for picnicking in the park.
4. The **noisome** fumes arising from mixing chlorine and ammonia produce chlorine gas and can be fatal.
5. It is so **noisy** in that nightclub that you can't hear the band, and the place reeks with the **noisome** stale smell of tobacco.
6. A snake crawled out of the **noisome** decaying swamp.
7. Some people prefer a **noisy**, congested city to the peace and quiet of the country.
8. As we approached the deserted cabin, a **noisome** smell assailed our nostrils.

## OPHTHALMOLGIST, OPTICIAN, OPTOMETRIST

1. Take this lens prescription to an **optician**, who will be able to make prescription sunglasses for you.
2. The **ophthalmologist** used laser surgery to repair the patient's torn retina.
3. My **ophthalmologist** called in a prescription for eyedrops that treat cataracts in the hopes of avoiding cataract surgery.
4. An **optometrist** is not a physician but is, nevertheless, the main provider of such eye care as giving eye exams and diagnosing vision problems.
5. I'd take your eyeglasses to an **optician** to have that scratched lens replaced.

6. My local **optometrist** gave me an eye exam and offered a large assortment of eyeglass frames for me to choose from.
7. The **ophthalmologist** routinely schedules operations to correct glaucoma on Wednesdays and Fridays.
8. You had better have your irritated eye checked by an **ophthalmologist** to make sure you don't have an infection from contaminated contact lens solution.
9. I need to see an **optometrist** to get a new prescription for a pair of eyeglasses.
10. Eye injuries should be referred to an **ophthalmologist** to ensure there is no infection.
11. Tracy took her young daughter to an **optician** to be fitted for glasses.
12. You need to be checked by an **ophthalmologist** to make sure you don't have an eye infection.

## PASSED, PAST
1. Had she driven **past** that same house sometime in the **past**?
2. A week had **passed** since he **passed** his driver's test, and still — no ticket!
3. In the **past**, the senator would have had no trouble having her resolution **passed**, but now she was not so sure. Had her popularity **passed**?
4. A month had **passed** since he had received her letter.
5. J.S. Bach **passed** on his musical ability to his son.
6. I think my electric bill is now **past** due.
7. She accelerated and **passed** the tractor trailer.
8. A few moments **passed** before anyone spoke.
9. I'm afraid it's **past** the deadline to enroll.
10. It is time for you to stop thinking about the **past** and plan for your future.
11. She avoided his eyes as she walked **past** him.

12. Suddenly a troubling thought **passed** through Vanessa's mind.
13. Had her **past** indiscretions found her out and were they resurfacing?
14. So many years had **passed**, and all that was in the **past**, wasn't it?
15. Surely Kyle wouldn't have **passed** her letters on to Lisle, would he?
16. That would be **past** belief!
17. She had trusted Kyle completely in the **past**.
18. Had all his feeling for her now **passed**?
19. The possibility that her **past** lover had betrayed her was too much to face.
20. Vanessa felt her knees crumple beneath her, and she **passed** out.

## PRINCIPAL, PRINCIPLE
1. What is your **principal** reason for deciding to resign?
2. The school **principal** believed that the **principle** of free speech did not give students the right to openly insult teachers.
3. What is the difference between following the **principle** of the law and following the "letter of the law"?
4. It may be the **principle** of gravity that is the **principal** cause of wrinkles and sagging skin attributed to age.
5. The irrational **principle** upon which your argument is based is my **principal** objection to it.

## PRONE, SUPINE
1. She assumed a **prone** position to do push-ups.
2. I am **prone** to sleep on my back, **supine**.
3. He lay down on the weight bench **supine** and raised the weights above his head.
4. Harry is **prone** to be **supine,** that is, to take the path of least effort and resistance.

5. If you lie **prone**, it will be it easier to find your contact lens on the floor.
6. They lay **supine**, watching for falling stars.
7. Being overtired makes him **prone** to errors.

## QUALIFY, QUANTIFY

1. How can one give a number to, or **quantify**, the impact and relevance of this research?
2. The number of years it takes for babies' names to rise and then fall in popularity helps us to **quantify** how long fads last.
3. What must I do in order to **qualify** as a contestant on your TV game show?
4. We conducted the survey to **quantify** the effects of our new advertising campaign.
5. It is not possible to **quantify**, or put a measure to, the value of love or of friendship or of loyalty.
6. How can I find out if I **qualify** for disability benefits?
7. To **qualify** for membership in Mensa International you need only score in the top 2% of the population on an approved intelligence test.
8. Is an intelligence test, such as the Stanford-Binet, a reliable means to **quantify** intelligence?

## REIGN, REIN

1. She pulled back on the **reins**, trying to get control of the horse, but could not **rein** him in.
2. How long do you think his **reign** as world champion will last?
3. Peace would **reign** for forty-seven years during the **reign** of the pharaoh.
4. She was given free **rein** to do whatever she thought necessary to save the company.
5. He gave his horse the **reins** and galloped to the finish line.
6. In the third year of her **reign** there was a revolt.

7. What will it take to make him **rein** in his temper?
8. To start up a canter from a walk, pull up on the curb **rein** a little and turn the head slightly right.
9. The teacher managed the horse with a leading **rein** until he could entrust his pupil with the **reins.**
10. The two rulers could no longer **reign** together
11. During the **reign** of King George III, Parliament made attempts to **rein** in the rebellious American colonists, without success.
12. In 1776, during the **reign** of Louis XVI of France, Benjamin Franklin charmed the French court and won a sizable loan for the American army.
13. The hapless King Charles II was to **reign** over England in what was arguably its worst year in history, 1666, the year of the great fire of London, in which 80% of the city burned down.
14. This **reign** of fire raged for five days, and even months afterwards, small fires continued to burn throughout the city.
15. Frantic attempts to **rein** in the fire were futile.
16. The catastrophe did, however, succeed in putting an end to the **reign** of the city's vast rat population.
17. So many rats and their resident fleas perished in the blaze, that it effectively put an end to the **reign** of the Black Death, or Great Plague, in that beleaguered city.
18. Afterwards, officials were kept busy trying to **rein** in citizens trying to lynch French catholic extremists (whom they blamed for the fire, whose real cause was sparks from the oven of the King's royal baker).

**RESTFUL, RESTIVE**
1. Cruising down the river on a Sunday afternoon can be a relaxing, **restful** experience for some, but can make those of a more restless, impatient disposition **restive** and irritable.

2. Concerned that the prisoners were growing **restive,** prison authorities tried piping in soothing, **restful** music.
3. When the weather prevented children from going outside for recess, they became increasingly **restive** and difficult to teach.
4. Green and blue are **restful** colors, but when their walls are painted screaming pink or flamboyant orange, residents become **restive**.
5. After supervising rambunctious third-graders on a trip to the zoo, I looked forward to the **restful** calm of my quiet apartment.
6. Her horse was getting **restive** and pawed the ground.
7. Let's spend a **restful** day in the country.

## SET, SIT

1. Make sure all the troublemakers **sit** in the first row, where you can see them, and never let Mark **sit** next to Dennis!
2. Be very careful when you **set** down that liquid.
3. Just **set** your books on the counter and **sit** down.
4. If you **set** your package on the floor, someone will be able to **sit** in that seat.
5. If you **set** the TV on the kitchen shelf, we'll be able to **sit** and watch it as we eat.

## SHALL, WILL

1. We **shall** go to the cabin tomorrow if you **will** agree to meet us there.
2. No, I absolutely **will** not do what you ask, and never mention it again!
3. They **shall** follow the regulations or I'll see them in court!
4. He **will** arrive in New York at 6:30.
5. I **will** not go to Los Angeles, and there's no way you can make me; I **shall** think about a trip to Las Vegas, however.
6. They said they **will** be here in time for supper.
7. We **shall** be at the exit in ten minutes.

8. I certainly **will** leave to join the circus, no matter how much you object!
9. You **shall** turn down that music, if you know what's good for you!
10. If it is meant to be, it **will** be.
11. **Shall** we go now during the intermission, or would you prefer to stay?
12. I'm busy right now, but I **shall** have time to meet with you tomorrow afternoon.
13. Believe me, he **shall** be punished for his crime!
14. You **shall** do it, if you know what's good for you!
15. What **shall** we do if it rains?
16. It **will** be disastrous if we miss our flight!
17. Where **shall** we eat tonight?

## STATIONARY, STATIONERY

1. Now that I've named my company, I must design **stationery** and business cards.
2. As a musician, I constantly traveled, but now I finally have a **stationary** home next to a **stationery** store.
3. I understand, however, that the **stationery** store is about to move—if a **stationary** (or **stationery**) store can move, that is.
4. During the earthquake, **stationery**, coffee cups, and pens flew off the desk, which remained **stationary**, since it was bolted to the floor.
5. Her beliefs never ever wavered and were as unmovable and **stationary** as the giant and noble trees she vowed to protect.
6. "Never, never will I buy **stationery** made from any but recycled paper!" she vowed.

## THAN, THEN

1. He seems to think he is better **than** anyone else.
2. Less **than** a month later, another hurricane struck.

3. Just **then** a stranger came running through the woods towards them.
4. Are you better off **than** you were a year ago?
5. We can't go back for your vitamins because **then** we would miss the train.
6. I was an accountant, but since **then** I have left my job and become a self-published author.
7. Of all romances in history, few were more tempestuous **than** that of Napoleon Bonaparte and Josephine.
8. Napoleon had never been more smitten **than** when he met the beautiful Paris socialite, a widow, who was **then** thirty-two years old.
9. Josephine at first evaded his advances, but **then** relented, and they were married in 1796.
10. Napoleon **then** went on military campaigns.
11. Rather **than** brood over his absence, Josephine **then** attended to her own affairs, adulterous though they were.
12. On hearing about her conduct, the enraged Napoleon **then** demanded a divorce.
13. But when Josephine pleaded with him, he ended up forgiving, rather **than** divorcing, her.
14. They did not **then** live happily ever after, for when Napoleon became emperor, he divorced Josephine, hoping for a son.
15. He married a woman who was much younger **than** Josephine and who did **then** bear him a son.
16. Josephine died while Napoleon was in exile; he **then** escaped and returned to Paris.
17. The grief-stricken Napoleon **then** picked violets from Josephine's garden and put them in a locket, which he **then** wore until his death.
18. Napoleon loved no woman more **than** Josephine.

**THEIR, THERE. THEY'RE**
1. **They're** on **their** way and should be here soon.

2. **There** are only a few who disagreed with **their** decision.
3. Is that **their** dog over **there** by the barn?
4. If **they're** sure they put **their** lunch **there** on the picnic table, what became of it?
5. **They're** claiming that is not **their** baseball over **there** by the broken window.
6. **There** are millions of Monopoly® fans worldwide, but **they're** largely unaware that **their** favorite board game helped Allied POWs escape from Nazi prison camps thanks to the British Secret Service and **their** Operation Monopoly.
7. The Brits had a company making silk escape maps carried by **their** airmen.
8. The factory-made Monopoly® games **there**, as well.
9. Maps and Monopoly® — **they're** unlikely candidates to be paired in a secret service plot. Not so.
10. **Their** plan was to hide escape maps and tools inside the game boxes and smuggle them into German prison camps along with Red Cross packages sent **there**.
11. They marked **their** "special edition" games with a red dot in the FREE PARKING space.
12. **Their** boxes were altered with carefully cut holes and slots.
13. **There** were extra playing pieces: a file, compass, and silk escape map specific to the region and showing the "safe houses."
14. **There** was real foreign currency to be used as bribes under the Monopoly® money.
15. To be compliant with the Geneva Convention, the Nazis distributed Red Cross packages and the Monopoly® games to **their** prisoners.
16. Some 35,000 Allied prisoners escaped German prison camps. How many owed **their** escape to the game of Monopoly®?

## TO, TOO, TWO
1. Did you ever feel **too** tired **to** go **to** bed?
2. I received **two** dollars **too** much in change.
3. I only had **two** hours of sleep — far **too** little.
4. **Two** desserts are **two too** many for me!
5. Let's go **to** Texas **two** by **two**.
6. Elvis Presley was no stranger **to** guns.
7. In 1970 Elvis went **to** the White House unannounced **to** petition Richard Nixon **to** appoint him as an undercover agent.
8. He wanted **to** investigate drug abuse and Communist brainwashing techniques **too**.
9. Elvis went prepared. He packed **two** handguns, one for himself, the other **to** give **to** Nixon, who might need protection, **too**.
10. Not **to** be outdone, Nixon gave a gift **to** Presley — a Special Assistant badge from the Bureau of Narcotics and Dangerous Drugs.
11. The FBI got into the act, **too**, and gave Presley permits **to** carry firearms in every state **to** assist him in pursuing his undercover work.
12. Elvis kept his firearms readily available at home in Graceland, **too**.
13. He was known **to** shoot his TV set whenever Mel Torme came on the screen.
14. He accorded this treatment to Robert Goulet, **too,** when Goulet appeared on TV.
15. Elvis's car, **too**, fell victim **to** his gun-toting temper.
16. When his car refused **to** start, he shot it.

## UNDO, UNDUE
1. I regret the **undue** harshness of my remarks and wish I could **undo** them.
2. Although it is not possible to **undo** the actions of the past, it is possible to give them **undue** attention.

3. It is not possible to **undo** the knots in this tangled mass of marionette strings without spending **undue** time and effort.
4. If only it were possible to **undo** my actions.
5. Please help your little brother **undo** his shoelaces.
6. It was not possible to **undo** what he had done without **undue** expense and effort.
7. Be careful about appearing over-eager or of showing **undue** enthusiasm because you will run the risk of seeming unsophisticated.
8. If you change your attitude and henceforth refrain from **undue** criticism of your partner, you can **undo** the damage done to your relationship.

## VAIN, VEIN

1. Those are **vain** promises, without substance.
2. The prospectors struck a **vein** of silver.
3. In a more serious **vein**, here are the latest figures on inflation.
4. Alvin's three previous attempts to pass his driver's test were in **vain**.
5. The nurse drew blood from a **vein** in his left arm.
6. Although quite beautiful, she was not **vain** about her appearance.

## WAS, WERE

1. She **was** surprised to see there **were** only a few customers in the diner.
2. If I **were** you, I would order a salad instead.
3. I think it **was** Robin Williams who said, "If you **were** right, I'd agree with you."
4. When you **were** in Hoboken, I **was** in Hackensack.
5. It **was** fate. You and I **were** in the right place, and it **was** the right time.
6. You **were** gorgeous and I **was** rich.

7. Together we **were** perfect.
8. What **was** it the poet wrote . . . something about if paradise **were** now?
9. Oh, if only I **were** a poet and my words **were** poems!
10. Whether we **were** fools or dreamers matters not.
11. We **were** in love. Or, if it **was** not love, it **was** something quite like it.
12. **Was** it to last? Alas, life is not perfect. If only it **were**!


## WEATHER, WHETHER

1. I don't know **whether** to wash the car today or wait until the weather cooperates.
2. Grit your teeth and **weather** the storm, **whether** or not ywhicou're frightened.
3. No matter **whether** it rains, sleets, or snows, you know you'll have **weather**.
4. They say Los Angeles never has **weather**, but I don't know **whether** or not I agree with that.
5. It doesn't matter **whether** the **weather** is good or bad, everybody talks about it.


## WHO, WHICH, THAT

1. I wonder **who** planted the daffodils **that** have sprung up along the barnyard fence.
2. I used to live in Talbott, **which** is a small town in East Tennessee.
3. One of my friends in our local book club recommended **that** historical novel to me.
4. Joan found a realtor **who** helped her sell her house, **which** was a brick rancher **that** had a heated pool.
5. Claude is the only one **who** could have known what happened on **that** fateful day.

6. Judo is not an activity **that** one usually associates with presidents.
7. Yet our 26th president, **who** was Theodore Roosevelt, was a judo enthusiast.
8. Theodore Roosevelt earned a distinction **that** was unique, one **that** few have ever heard about.
9. He was America's first Brown Belt in Judo, **which** is a sport of unarmed combat **that** was derived from jujitsu.
10. Roosevelt practiced judo in the White House basement, **which** he covered with training mats.
11. He practiced judo with anyone **who** was available, including his wife and sister-in-law.
12. Once during an official White House lunch, **which** was unsurprisingly boring, he threw the visiting Swiss minister to the floor and demonstrated a hold **that** he learned in judo.
13. This boisterous activity was a diversion **that** delighted his other guests, although probably not the one **who** brushed himself off a*s he got up from the floor.
14 The president's popularity, **which** was great, was bolstered further when he went hunting in Mississippi and refused to shoot a black bear cub.
15. This story, **which** touched America's heart, had an interesting result.
16. People began naming their stuffed toy bears "Teddy," **which** is a name **that** has stuck.

## WHO, WHOM
1. Did you see **who** left the package at the door?
2. To **whom** is the package addressed, and **who** is the sender?
3. Ralph, **who** first noticed the suspicious package, is not one **who** is easily rattled. He is, however, someone **who** easily leaps to false conclusions, and to **whom** a number of false alarms in the form of 911 calls have been attributed.

Perhaps this is only to be expected from one **who** devours spy novels and tales of espionage. He is a person for **whom** I have the utmost respect and **whom** I hold in deepest regard. Yet Ralph is someone **who** prefers to live life as fiction, someone **who** likes to believe that behind every occurrence lurks a spy.

## WHO'S, WHOSE

1. **Who's** the teacher **who's** been the most influential in your life?
2. It was Mr. Gillespie **whose** words inspired me and **who's** always been a role model for me.
3. He's one of those people **whose** face is familiar but **whose** name escapes me.
4. **Who's** the author of that book about Captain Ahab, **whose** nemesis is a giant white whale?
5. **Who's** got a suggestion on a good book to read at the beach?
6. I want one **whose** plot is thrilling, a real page-turner.

## YOUR, YOU'RE

1. Let a smile be **your** umbrella on a rainy day; for when **you're** smiling, the whole world smiles with you.
2. What is that song **you're** singing?
3. Is that song "**You're** No One If **You're** Not on Twitter"? Or is it, "If **You're** Happy and You Know It, Clap **Your** Hands"?
4. I guess **you're** tone deaf. Actually, I was singing, "**You're** Going to Get **Your** Fingers Burnt."
5. That song is my second favorite song after "**You're** So Vain."
6. If **your** tastes run to Country Western, try, "When You Leave, Walk Out Backwards So I'll Think **You're** Walking In."

7. Or you might like one of these: "You Can't Have **Your** Kate and **Your** Edith Too" or "My John Deere Was Breaking **Your** Field, While **Your** Dear John Was Breaking My Heart."
8. If you like those, I'd recommend, "Am I Double Parked by the Curbstone of **Your** Heart?"
9. One of my all-time favorites is: "You Changed **Your** Name from Brown to Jones, and Mine from Brown to Blue."

## TRICKY SINGULARS & PLURALS

1. The entertainment, provided by **alumni** and **alumnae**, consisted of two **concerti** (or **concertos**) for oboe and three short **tableaux** (or **tableaus**) in which the performers took on the **personae** (or **personas**) of **cherubim** (or **cherubs**) and **seraphim** (or **seraphs**).
2. After multiple **analyses** of **data** according to agreed-on **criteria**, we were able to reject **hypotheses** whose **bases** rested on defective **schemata**.
3. If you could examine the **corpora** of the following life forms, which could contain all three of these structures — 1. cerebral **cortices** (or **cortexes**); 2. **testes**; and 3. **vertebrae** (or **vertebras**): **algae** (or **algas**), **bacteria**, **viruses**, **fungi** (or **funguses**), **hippopotamuses** (or **hippopotami**), **larvae** (or **larvas**), **octopuses** (or **octopi**), and **platypuses** (or **platypusi**)?
4. After sharing **gateaux** and **matzoth** (or **matzos**) with their former **beaux** (or **beaus**), Adele and Jeannine said their **adieus** (or **adieux**) and bravely traversed the river's raging **vortices** (or **vortexes**) to return to their respective **châteaus** (or **châteaux**) on the **vertexes** (or **vertices**) of adjoining mountains, where they contemplated their **trousseaux** (or **trousseaus**), stored in massive mahogany **bureaus** (or **bureaux**).
5. The **Burgesses**, who delighted in **minutiae**, sought to improve their respective **IQs** by finding errors in **encyclopedias**, recording them in **memorandums** (or

281

**memoranda**), and submitting them to publishers' **editor-in-chiefs** as **errata** — or to the **media** (or **mediums**), if publishers made the mistake of ignoring them.

Author's Note

Dear Reader,

Thank you for choosing WORD SAVVY HANDBOOK: USE THE RIGHT WORD If you enjoyed the book and found it useful, I'd like to ask a favor. Would you leave a short review on Amazon.com?

Reviews are incredibly helpful in helping others find new books, and they take just a moment to leave.

Just go to the book's page on Amazon.com and scroll down. Click on "WRITE A CUSTOMER REVIEW." This will take you straight to the review page, where you can check your STAR rating for the book and leave a comment.

Thank you so much. Authors really appreciate reviews, and I would love to get your feedback.

Happy writing!

# Nancy Ragno

**email:** wordsavvyhandbook@gmail.com
**Twitter:** @savvy_be

# Index

accept, 8
access, 188
addenda, addendum, 218
aieu, adieus, adieux, 218
adverse, 188
alga, algae, 218
a lot, 24
a while, 31
acute,10
addendum, 218
adieu, 218
adieus, adieux, 218
advice, 12
advise,12, 188
affect, 14
aggravate,16
alga, 218
algae, 218
alibi,18, 188
all ready, 20
all together, 22
allot, 24
alot, 24, 208
already,20
alright, 209
altercation, 187
altogether, 22
alumna, 218
alumnae, 218
alumni, 219

alumnus, 219
ambivalent, 189
among, 26
analyses, 218
analysis, 218
Answers, 241-286
antenna, 218
antennae, 218
anxious, 189
anyways, 208
appendices, 218
appendix, 218
as if, 123
as, 123
assure, 29
Author's Note, 293
automaton, 218
awhile,31
axes, 218
axis, 218
bacteria, 219
bacterium 219
bad, 33
badly, 33
bases, 218
basis, 218
beâu, 218
beâux, 218
beg the question, 210
between, 26
bi-,189
brake, 36

break, 36
bring, 38
bureau, 219
bureaux, 219
bursted, 210
cacti, 219
cactus, 219
can, 40
capital, 42
capitol, 42
censor, 44
censure, 44
chateâu, 219
chateâux, 219
cherub, 219
cherubini, 219
chord, 47
chronic, 10
cite, 49
coarse, 52
compare, 54,190
compendious, 191
complement, 56
compliment,56
compose, 58
compound nouns,
plfur222
comprise,58
concerti, 219
concerto, 219
confused, words
  4-185
connote, 60
consequent, 191
continual, 62

continuous, 62
contrast,54
cord, 47
corpora, 219
corpus, 219
cortices, 219
could care less, 209
could of, 2ll
council, 64
counsel, 64
course, 52
crises, 219
crisis, 219
criteria, 219
criterion, 219
curricula, 219
curriculum, 219
data, 219
datum, 219
denote, 60,191
desert, 66
dessert, 66
device, 68
devise, 68
diagnoses, 219
diagnosis, 219
diffuse, 192
diligency, 211
disinterested, 70
dogma, 219
dogmata, 219
downgrade, 192
due to, 192
e.g., 72
economic, 193

effect, 14
elicit, 74
ellipses, 219
ellipsis, 219
emigrate, 76
empathy, 78
emphases, 219
emphasis, 219
encyclopedia, 219
enervate, 193
ensure, 29
errata, 219
erratum, 218
escape goat, 211
etc., 194
every day, 80
every one, 82
everyday, 80
everyone, 82
except, 8
excuse, 8
farther, 84
fastly, 220
fewer, 86
final ultimatum, 211
fluke, 194
focuses, 219
focus, 219
for all intensive
  purposes, 211
foreign, singulars and
  plurals 218
foreword, 88
formally, 90
formerly, 90

formula, 219
formulae, 219
fortuitous, 92
fortunate, 92
forum, 219
forward, 88
fungi, 219
fungus, 219
further, 84
gateâu, 220
gateâux, 220
genera, 220
genus, 220
good, 94
gourmand, 194
hanged, 96
have your cake and
  eat it too, 212
healthful, 98
healthy, 98
heartwrenching, 211
hippopotamus, 220
hippopotami, 220
historic, 100
historical, 100
hone in on, 211
honoraria, 221
honorarium, 220
hung, 96
hypotheses, 220
hypothesis, 220
I, 102
i.e., 72
ignorant, 211
illicit, 74

immigrate, 76
imply, 104
index, 220
indices, 220
infamous, 195
infer, 104
ingenuous, 195
insure, 29
ironic, 196
irregardless, 212
irritate, 16
Plurits, 106
it's, its,106
jealous, 108
judicial, 110
judicious, 110
key, 112
kibbutz, 220
kibbutzim, 220
larva, 220
larvae, 220
lay, 114
lead, 117
leave, 120
led, 117
less, 86
let, 120
lie, 114
like, 123
limpid, 196
literally. 196
loci, locus, 220
loose, 126
lose, 126
matrices, 220

matrix, 220
matzo, 220
matzoth, 220
maxima, 220
maximum, 220
may, 40,128
me, 102
media 220
medium, 220
memoranda, 220
memorandum, 220
might, 128
millennia, 220
millennium, 220
minima, 220
minimum, 220
minutia, 220
minutiae, 220
misspelled words, 228
misused words, 205
mitigate, 196
mitzvah, 221
mitzvoth, 221
morbid, 197
mute, 197
nauseous, 212
naval, 130
navel, 130
nemesis, 197
noisome, 132
noisy, 132
nonplussed, 198
nuclei, nucleus, 221
-octopus, 221
octopuses, 221

odious, 198
officious, 199
ophthalmologist,134
optician, 134
optometrist, 134
orientated, 212
parentheses, 222
parenthesis, 222
passed, 137
past, 137
peaceable, 199
penultimate, 199
persona, 221
personae, 221
peruse, 200
phenomena, 221
phenomenon, 221
plateau, 221
plateaux, 221
platypus, 221
platypuses, 221
plethora, 200
plurals 215-227
plurals, foreign
  218-222
plurals, proper nouns,
  234
plurals, numbers &
  numerals, 234
practicable, 200
precedence, 201
principal, 140
principle,140
pristine, 201
progenitor, 201

prone, 142
proper, letters, 226
proper names, 226
proper numbers, 226
qualify, 144
quantify, 144
quay, 102, 189
quicker, 212
radii, 222
radius, 222,
random, 202
redundant, 202
referenda, 221
referendum, 221
reign, 146
rein, 146
reiterate, 212
reoccurrence, 212
restful,149
restive, 149, 203
schema, 221
schemata, 221
Scotch, 213
seasonable, 203
semi-, 189
seraph, 221
seraphim, 221
set, 151
shall, 153
sight, 49
singulars, 216
sit, 151
site, 49
spelling demons, 228
stadia, 221

stadium, 221
stationary, 156
stationery, 15
statue of limitations, 213
stigma, 221
stigmata, 221
stimuli, 221
stimulus, 221
stoma, 221
stomata, 221
strata. 221
stratum, 221
syllabus, 221
syllabi, 221
supine, 142
suppose to, 215
sympathy,78
symposia, 222
symposium, 221
synopsis, 221
synopses, 221
syntheses, 222
synthesis, 222
tableau, 222
tableaux, 222
take, 38
tantamount, 204
testes, 222
testis, 222
than, 158
that, 176
their, 161
then, 158
there, 161

theses, 223
thesis, 223
they're,161
to,164
too,164
trousseau, 223
trousseaux, 223
two, 164
ultimata, 223
ultimatum, 223
undo, 167,204
undue, 167, 204
uninterested, 70
vain, 169
vein, 169
verse, 204
vertebra, 223
vertebrae. 223
vertex, 223
vertices, 223
virus, 223
vortices, 223
vortex, 223
was, 171
weather, 174
well, 94
were, 171
whether, 174
which, 176
who, 176, 179
whom, 179
who's, 181
whose, 181
will, 153
wrongful, 205

your, 183
you're, 183
zealous,108

*The difference between the almost right word and the right word is really a large matter — 'tis the difference between the lightning bug and the lightning.*

*— Mark Twain*

*The six most important words:*
"I admit I made a mistake."

*The five most important words:*
"You did a good job."

*The four most important words:*
"What is your opinion?"

*The three most important words:*
"If you please."

*The two most important words:*
"Thank you'

*The one least important word,*
"I."

— *Anonymous*